D0626549

CLICK.OLOGY

CLICK.OLOGY

What works in online shopping
and how your business can use
consumer psychology to succeed

GRAHAM JONES

NICHOLAS BREALEY
PUBLISHING
London • Boston

First published by
Nicholas Brealey Publishing in 2014

3–5 Spafield Street
Clerkenwell, London
EC1R 4QB, UK
Tel: +44 (0)20 7239 0360
Fax: +44 (0)20 7239 0370

20 Park Plaza
Boston
MA 02116, USA
Tel: (888) BREALEY
Fax: (617) 523 3708

www.nicholasbrealey.com
click.ology.biz

ISBN: 978-1-85788-604-7
eISBN: 978-1-85788-930-7

British Library Cataloguing in Publication Data
A catalogue record for this book is available from the
British Library.

Printed in Finland by Bookwell.

CONTENTS

INTRODUCTION

Shopping online is a regular activity for millions of people around the world. In 2012, more than $1 trillion was spent on goods in online retail – that's before you even consider the amount spent on booking travel tickets, or buying business services such as accountancy, legal advice, or consultancy. Around 10% of all worldwide shopping is online, with predictions that this will double by 2015. In fact, the global economy now depends on internet shopping of all kinds.

Until recently, the US dominated online retail, but gradually other parts of the world are catching the bug. In Europe, about 10% of all retail is online, and the UK tops the league table with 13%. Meanwhile, the Asia Pacific region has come to represent a third of all online buying. By 2016, it is predicted that 40% of online sales will be conducted there, with Europe representing only half that amount.

Yet in spite of – or perhaps because of – the billions of dollars, euros, yen, rubles, rupees, pesos, or pounds being spent online, the world of shopping is at a crossroads, with many traditional, established businesses discovering that what has worked for so long offline does not work online, and that what works online does not necessarily translate offline: that what they are doing simply does not "click." To make matters worse, there is little in the way of solid advice on how to make sure an online shop functions effectively and efficiently. This book is designed to fill that practical knowledge gap. But it is also about the psychology behind online shopping, so it will appeal to the interested consumer as well as the business owner, retailer, or marketer.

Drawing on my 15 years' experience as a specialist in internet psychology – during which I've been getting to know how people behave online and analyzing web-based customer behavior – this book will offer you a peek inside an online shopper's mind, revealing the subconscious aspects of a website and how you as a business owner, retailer, or marketer can consciously make customers feel involved. The ideas in this book also map onto my five-step

CLICK system, which will ensure that your online store is focused on both the practical and psychological needs of your customers – that it is Convenient, Likeable, Informative, Customized, and Knowledgeable.

Whether you're running the website of a small business or a large corporation, whether you're involved purely online or in a mixture of on- and offline, this book will demonstrate what works online. It will help you understand and connect with your customers, ensuring that you provide an internet retail experience that works for them – and for you.

I begin by looking at why people shop, online or offline. Indeed, throughout this book I expose the similarities and the differences between the way we shop online and the way people buy in the "real world," and what we can learn from this. In both situations, customers rarely buy things because they have to. As Chapter 1 reveals, most people go shopping for psychological reasons, or simply because they want to be sociable. Shopping is much less about "buying" and much more about "being."

But why should people shop online? In Chapter 2, I look at the reasons many people specifically prefer online shopping to real-world, offline buying. Much of the discussion about online shopping has centered on the superficial convenience it provides, yet the real motivation goes much deeper than this. As this chapter demonstrates, people prefer online shopping because it offers control and the promise of real choice. These are powerful psychological motivators.

What is more, the practicalities of how we shop online are also far from straightforward. They are covered in Chapter 3, which explains that even though there are all sorts of potential pathways and routes through an online shop, the retailer has less than a few seconds to engage a shopper's attention: one click and they're gone. The impact of new devices such as tablets also means that shoppers are behaving differently online to even just a couple of years ago. For instance, they can now shop anywhere – on the train, in a bus queue, or down the pub – and that means they are buying much more on a whim than ever before.

One significant focus for online shoppers is pricing. The internet has enabled comparison shopping in ways that simply cannot be done easily in the real world. In Chapter 4 I look at the psychology of pricing and demonstrate how sometimes the "obvious" way to price online products and services is far from the most effective.

One of the reasons online retailers do not sell as much as they would like is shopping cart abandonment. People fill up their online shopping baskets and then, just as they're about to pay, they change their mind and leave the website. One of the main factors behind this frustrating phenomenon is unexpected payment issues, which I explore in Chapter 5, as well as offering advice on how to learn from the principles of offline retail and thereby maximize sales.

Internet shoppers do like to be in control and therefore often want to send goods back. Online shops that have the easiest ways of returning things are those that are doing well. Chapter 6 considers whether the only real differentiator between online stores is the level of customer service provided, of which a simple returns system is only one aspect.

Equally important to online shoppers is the need to buy things their friends like, and to be *seen* to be buying things other people will like. The social side of shopping is often underestimated, yet it is a powerful motivator for buying. In Chapter 7, I explain why websites that offer an involved, social experience are likely to be those that succeed the most. Nevertheless, there is a downside to this – get your customer service even slightly wrong and your shoppers will be quick to pronounce judgment on you via their social networks.

Another key issue, which arises repeatedly in my discussions with retailers, is the need to establish immediate trust. Perceptive internet shoppers look for signs that they can trust your online store; if they cannot find them, they leave within seconds. Unlike real-world shops, you don't have the time online to establish a relationship with customers through chitchat: people look for immediate, visible signs of trust, which Chapter 8 explores how to create. Reviews, ratings, and trade badges are all important – but the one element that online shoppers look for first is the one that most retailers forget. This chapter shows you what that is.

Of course, trust in an individual store is one thing, but online shoppers also need to trust the internet as a whole. Internet shoppers have been victims of fraud, theft of credit card details, and a host of other activities that reduce people's confidence in buying from the web. In Chapter 9 I explore the ways in which unscrupulous internet traders are eroding trust in the entire ecommerce world and how you can set yourself apart from the "bad boys."

Each chapter includes advice and tips on how your online business can tap into the psychological aspects of retail, and most feature a "blueprint" of what you need to do to ensure your online shop works in the best possible way. Chapter 10 draws on these blueprints to detail the essential steps to creating the perfect online store.

But where does the future of retail lie? Some analysts suggest that online shopping is going to become the norm, with billions of people preferring to shop online for almost everything they need. Others contend that we will become fed up with hidden costs, or poor implementation of technology, and will go back to real-world shopping. However, as I describe in Chapter 11, if online can learn from offline and vice versa, both can thrive in the fast-changing retail environment. On the other hand, if businesses fail to keep themselves open to change and don't continue to adapt, whether they are on- or offline they will not survive. To help you, Chapter 12 sums up how to use the CLICK system to be truly effective online.

As a business owner or retailer – large or small – or someone who works as a marketer in the web department of an organization, you can dip in and out of this book and read selected chapters if you wish. The same is true if you are interested in the world of online consumer psychology or in how the retail landscape is changing. However, if you are a business owner, retailer, or marketer, you are going to gain the greatest benefit if you actually use the information contained throughout the book. Your customers do not focus on only one aspect of their engagement with your online shop – they absorb the whole experience. As a result, focusing on only one or two chapters in this book is going to lead to only a limited impact. Even so, sometimes that limited impact can be transforming. I suggested to one client that they should change just one thing on their website and doing so revolutionized their sales.

If they were able to gain that much from the advice in one chapter, just think of the benefits if you read the whole book.

If your business can tap into the experience and psychology of both online and offline retail, applying the principles of the CLICK system, then it will be demonstrating true click.ology.

THE CLICK SYSTEM

Convenient

Convenience is not about "being online," it concerns a host of factors including your back-office processes. If these cause delays or issues, they can influence convenience for the customer. People perceive superficial convenience at a conscious level, looking at things like delivery terms or whether they can see a shopping cart. But their subconscious is also checking for deeper elements of convenience, including navigation, the perceived speed of the site, and the complexity of the language. The convenience of having a wide or highly relevant choice is also significant.

Likeable

How much do your customers like your store? Can they find their way around? Can they search for things easily? Is your site usable and accessible? Is the range of products extensive enough? Will people tell their friends about you? Are your policies and terms user-friendly? These are just some of the issues that make people like your store. If they don't like you or feel that you don't like them, they won't buy from you.

Informative

How much product information do you display? Can customers download data sheets or examples of packaging? Do you have articles about subjects relevant to your products? Customers use the web to seek out as much information as is relevant to them about potential purchases. If your website does not feature extensive information resources, you will miss out on sales.

Customized

How good is your online customer service? Can customers contact you when they want, in the way they want? Do you offer flexible delivery, on the customer's terms? Good online stores can do this and customers are starting to expect it.

Knowledgeable

When customers contact you, how good are your staff at answering their questions? Does your website show that you know your subject? Do you appear to be expert in your field? Customers are attracted to stores that demonstrate expertise, and thereby engender their trust.

1

WHY PEOPLE SHOP

As I sit writing these words a baby gorilla is staring right at me. Don't panic, it's not a real gorilla, it's a toy. Years ago, when I began my university studies into the human condition, I took a course on primatology, the study of primates like monkeys and gorillas. Part of the course included a day at the Zoological Society of London, where I came face to face with the most famous resident at Regent's Park, Guy the Gorilla. From that moment on, I simply adored these creatures, so when I saw this delightful 15 cm baby gorilla ornament I snapped it up. I didn't need a toy gorilla, of course – it was simply a "nice to have" – but I bought it nonetheless.

In contrast, last night I was cooking dinner with my 13-year-old son when we realized we were missing one of the ingredients in the recipe. When we'd gone shopping we had failed to buy something we needed – a "need to have."

You might think that people shop because we need things, but as these stories show, that is not necessarily the case. Often we buy things because we like them, and we frequently fail to buy the things we actually need. In this chapter I explore several different reasons for shopping, whether online or offline: shopping out of need, shopping out of desire, shopping because we are told to, and shopping to be social.

Shopping out of need

Clearly, we buy some things because we need them. For instance, we need to buy food and drink in order to survive. Some people around the world are self-sufficient, of course, growing their own food and rearing their own livestock, but in most nations with developed economies this is rare. Even if we buy direct from the farmer, rather than from a supermarket or corner store, we still have to shop for food.

Yet when we do shop for essentials, we often don't buy what we actually need. We are open to considerable persuasion to buy more than necessary, and to buy things we didn't even know we wanted. Indeed, perhaps 70% of what we buy in supermarkets world-wide represents unplanned purchases.[1] In his book *Consumer.ology*, Philip Graves recalls his discussions with women who routinely write shopping lists yet consistently forget to take the list to the shop with them.[2] This suggests that the list itself is not that import-ant and that even organized shoppers can easily be diverted, buying things that are not essential, that they do not need.

In addition, do we need the vast variety of choice available today? Take shoes as an example. You need to wear shoes of some sort, and you might require a variety of pairs for different functions: a smart pair for work, a pair for casual wear, something suitable for gardening, and another set for running. But consider the fact that Wikipedia lists 136 different major shoe brands, each of which offers dozens of styles and varieties. For trainers alone, in one sportswear shop I counted 200 different styles just on the "sale" shelves, with-out the hundreds of alternatives available at full price. The vast choice of styles and prices available in many products encourages us to buy more than just what we need, but what we like or desire as well.

The time we spend shopping is another indication of how we prioritize our buying activities. A study by GE Money discovered that British women spend almost 400 hours a year shopping, but less than a quarter of that time is spent on "essentials" – things they or their families really need.[3] The time we spend shopping for what we need is comparatively trivial, suggesting such things are of little interest or even relevance to us.

Almost all shopping is for things we do not need. Essentials are a tiny proportion of everything people buy.

Shopping out of desire

A study in Canada by BMO Financial Group found, for instance, that six out of every ten Canadians buy things they do not need, and that four out of ten buy things they never subsequently use.[4] Why? They do it to cheer themselves up. The study also uncovered the fact that, on average, Canadians spend $310 each month on items they desire but do not actually need. That's about 60% of all their shopping.

Canada could well represent the average of global shopping habits, located at number 27 in the top 50 nations analyzed for consumer spending by market research company Euromonitor. According to this analysis, Canadians spend around a third of their money on shopping. In Saudi Arabia shopping accounts for almost half of consumer spending, whereas in Singapore it is little more than one fifth; high property and transport prices mean that a greater proportion of spending goes on these items.[5] Yet even in Singapore, you cannot move in places like Orchard Road for fashion stores or jewelers tempting you to buy.

Travel across to Morocco and the souks of Marrakesh are doing just the same, putting piles of carpets or mountains of sweets out to tempt us, even if we have no actual desire to buy them. The world over, retailers are able to play on the fact that we tend to buy things we like on impulse.

This is to do with emotion. According to Dr. Ian Zimmerman, if you put something back on the shelf and decide not to buy it you are effectively "rejecting the idea that by purchasing that product you'll be happier, better respected, or more complete."[6] We buy things because we like them, but the process of liking something runs deeper than that. We feel an affinity or connection to the items we desire because by having them we feel good about ourselves. Part of this process is what the possession of the item does in terms of our identity.

Self-identity is a constant human struggle. It starts in childhood and then adapts in teenage years as we strive to establish who we are and how we stand out from other people. Yet at the same time, we have a real need to be accepted by others, to fit in. This leads to a conflict between the need to be individual and the need to be part of a group. Buying things can help resolve this tension. When we buy something we like it is often because we associate it with the kind of person we are. At the same time, the things we possess are like parts of our personality "uniform," acting as symbolic references to the kind of person we are and the kinds of groups with which we want to associate.

People buy things to show off their personality and establish their identity.

Consider Apple's iPhone. Research has discovered that people who display higher levels of extroversion in personality tests are more likely to own such a smartphone.[7] Companies that sell smartphones have used psychographic profiling so that they can match the person in the shop to the kind of phone they are most likely to desire. While the iPhone is a huge commercial success, you might be surprised to learn that most people do not actually want one. Indeed, in one study only one in three people in America wanted to get an iPhone.[8] The remaining two-thirds are not attracted to the phone because it does not match their personality. Not only do they prefer a different kind of phone, they don't need to be seen as part of the "iPhone club." However, people who do want to be part of that club – as part of their identity – simply "must" have an iPhone. It is a badge, a symbol that confirms "I am part of this tech-savvy group." When people feel part of a group, they feel better about themselves.

All of these factors mean that if your online shop focuses on people's wants, rather than needs, you are likely to gain additional sales. Amazon, for instance, does this using its recommendations system to provide customers with lists of things they are bound to like because they are similar to their previous purchases.

Shopping because we are told to

Much of the time we are not shopping for ourselves but on behalf of someone else. How many times have you been on your way out and your partner says, "While you are in town can you get...?" Family members can ask us, but so too can neighbors, friends, or work colleagues.

For retailers this can be incredibly frustrating. A customer meets a particular profile, so they know the kind of person they are dealing with, their habits and interests; then suddenly a particular customer buys something completely out of character. That's because they're not buying the item for themselves. This problem is exacerbated online, where it isn't possible to ask why a certain item has been purchased.

In a workshop I was running recently for a group of chief executives of medium-sized businesses, I was discussing the ability of a retailer such as Amazon to customize and personalize web pages with exactly the kinds of things each customer is interested in buying. Amazon does this with "cookies," small text files on your computer that help the site know who you are when you log in. Your identity can be matched with your purchasing patterns and your use of the website to provide suggested items. However, as the chief executives pointed out to me, this only works if you use Amazon solely for personal purchases. As soon as you start to buy presents or use the site to order for the needs of other members of your family, the recommendations Amazon makes become less personal. The system cannot account for the fact that you may be buying on someone else's behalf rather than for yourself, and the usual psychological hooks retailers might be able to apply, such as trying to trigger desire, will simply not work.

Say your partner has asked you to go to a fashion store and buy a scarf for their mother's birthday. You know which store to go to, the item you are looking for, and the color you need to pick out. As you don't wear scarves yourself, no amount of desire-based input from the shop will get you to buy more than what you came for. All of that promotional activity would be aimed at the kind of person for whom you are buying the scarf, not you. Because a sizable proportion of what consumers buy is not for them but for other people, this is an area of real difficulty for retailers to gain traction in.

> When people are shopping on behalf of other people, they
> are less prone to persuasion to buy other things.

When setting up your online shop, be aware that some people will
want to make quick buys, because they are purchasing on behalf
of someone else or they are simply shopping because they've been
told to get a specific item for their office or home. These shoppers
do not want to be faced with recommendations or additional items.
They simply want to go to your online store, find the item they're
looking for, and buy it, all in the minimum number of steps. UK
general-goods retailer Argos does this by allowing people to enter
an item number from its catalogue, which takes them straight to the
buying page for that specific product.

Shopping to be social

The fourth reason to shop is to spend time with other people.
Indeed, British retail entrepreneur Theo Paphitis said in an interview with the *Manchester Evening News* that shopping is a leisure
activity. However, he was not the first to point this out. As long ago
as 1726, Daniel Defoe wrote *The Complete English Tradesman*, in which
he discussed his observations of shopping. He wrote:

> *I have heard that some ladies, and those, too, persons of good note,
> have taken their coaches and spent a whole afternoon in Ludgate
> Street or Covent Garden, only to divert themselves in going from
> one mercer's shop to another, to look upon their fine silks, and to
> rattle and banter the journeymen and shopkeepers, and have not
> so much as the least occasion, much less intention, to buy anything;
> nay, not so much as carrying any money out with them to buy
> anything if they fancied it.*[9]

Retailers soon took advantage of the social side of shopping, building department stores so that people could look around, spend time
with friends, and stop and have tea or even a meal in the restaurant.
The first department store in the world was established in 1734 in

Derby, in the English Midlands. Called Bennets, it still trades on the site of the original premises. Meanwhile, in Sydney, Australia, the department store David Jones was established in 1838, and is the oldest shop of its kind still trading under the same name.[10] In the US, Macy's has been "the place to shop" in New York since 1858, and in Red Square, Moscow, GUM has been attracting shoppers since the late 1890s. Such stores have clearly stood the test of time and have one thing in common: they have social features at their heart.

When Harry Selfridge established his eponymous store in London's Oxford Street, he filled the shop with leisure options, including a writing room, a quiet room, and a library, as well as several restaurants. The aim was to make Selfridges a "destination" rather than a shop. This notion was continued by the use of the store as a place to host events, including the first public display of television in April 1925 by John Logie Baird.

Shopping malls and shopping centers continue to be leisure attractions. They have cinemas, restaurants, children's play areas, and entertainment in the lobbies. The Mall of America in Bloomington, Minnesota, one of the world's biggest shopping malls, includes the globe's largest indoor amusement park, an aquarium, a 13-story hotel, 14 cinemas, a train station, a comedy club, and 50 restaurants, in addition to its 520 shops, and hosts 400 annual events. It is so popular that it attracts 40 million visitors a year – that's more than twice the number who go to Disney's Magic Kingdom in Florida.

Even if we ignore vast malls such as this and venture onto Main Street or the High Street, there will be several coffee houses, bars, cafés, restaurants, and other meeting places nestled among the shops. Socialization is a key feature of shopping.

You can see this idea extended online, with people able to chat to their friends about what they have just bought by posting a notice on social media site Twitter or Facebook. Similarly, Instagram and Pinterest are full of people sharing images of their purchases.

I once spent several hours sitting in a cafeteria in the north of England, together with a couple of other psychologists, secretly observing the habits of shoppers who came in for a coffee. If people were on their own, they rarely opened their shopping bags to look at anything they had bought. But if they were with other people, they frequently took items out of their shopping bags to share their purchases with their friends. That's not a lot different to taking a picture and putting it on Facebook.

In a study of supermarket shoppers in Qatar, researchers were able to classify people into distinct groups according to their shopping behavior. Even in a supermarket, the two main behaviors were shopping for personal gratification and shopping to be social.[11] All of this shows that one of the benefits we get from shopping, on- or offline, is the trigger it provides for social engagement.

BLUEPRINT

It is important to understand the underlying reasons for people shopping. You need to provide an online shopping experience that connects with your customers at a fundamental psychological level.

1. Focus your online store on your customers' desires and wants, not necessarily needs.
2. Ensure that your shopping system allows for "quick buys," where people who know exactly what they want can purchase without fuss or diversion. This will ensure you meet the needs of people buying for someone else.
3. Provide social features in your store, making it easy for people to tell their friends what they have bought.

2

WHY PEOPLE SHOP ONLINE

The notion of shopping from a computer was pioneered by British inventor Michael Aldrich, who worked at Redifon Computers, later renamed Rediffusion. Aldrich's first client had been Thomson Holidays, which in 1981 managed to use computers to exchange telexes, the main way of confirming holiday bookings back then. Three years later, in June 1984, 72-year-old Mrs Jane Snowball bought some items from Tesco's supermarket in Gateshead, in the northeast of England,[1] using an electronic system connected to her telephone line and a television screen.

Almost a quarter of a century later, Aldrich's grandchildren wanted to know whether their granddad had really invented online shopping. Aldrich searched through his files and old papers, contacted some former work colleagues, and eventually pinned down the fact that Lawrence McGinty, then Science Editor of ITN (Independent Television News), had interviewed the first ever user of "teleshopping," as it was known then. Lawrence looked through the archives and found his interview with Jane Snowball, who admitted that even though the system was convenient, she missed being able to meet her friends at the local supermarket. Yet it was the convenience of electronic shopping that so interested the elderly people in Gateshead, because it meant they could get their groceries delivered more easily than by having to travel to the store. So McGinty had pinpointed what was to become one of online shopping's major benefits to consumers – convenience.

At the same time as the Tesco initiative was being piloted in the UK, US corporation CompuServe launched its "Electronic Mall" to 130,000 of its subscribers. The mall included 80 different suppliers who mainly provided a directory of products and a catalogue from which you could order using email. *Marketing News* magazine reported in November 1984 that the market for such a service was "relatively stagnant," essentially blaming a lack of technical skills among potential users.² The system showed the promise of what was to come, but lacked full convenience as it required users to be quite adept technically.

It was to be another decade before online shopping really started to take off. Up to this point the technology was slow and cumbersome, and it was only with the invention of the World Wide Web by Tim Berners-Lee in 1989, and his first website going live in 1991, that electronic shopping could become more useful. Even so, it was another three years before Pizza Hut became the first company to offer consumers the option to buy something online, with the launch of its web-based ordering system offering fast-food lovers a faster way of getting their dinner.

On April 27, 1995, the first book was sold securely online by WH Smith in London. Later that same year, Amazon opened its electronic doors to the public, and the internet quickly became established as a major commercial force. Through all these developments, however, the focus was always on convenience. The aim was to provide shopping facilities for people whenever they wanted, 24 hours a day, 7 days a week.

In a study conducted at the University of Wisconsin-Milwaukee, the notion of convenience was compared with the issue of risk when buying online.³ In many cases, the convenience outweighed the risk. People were prepared to take an increased risk – such as their credit card details being stored – in exchange for more convenience. The research also identified several aspects of convenience that were important to shoppers, including the ease with which orders could be placed compared with alternative methods such as over the telephone, the simplicity of payment, and the easy access to additional information about products.

> The human brain functions to make us do things with the least amount of effort. A desire for convenience is built in to humans as an ancient survival mechanism, helping us reduce effort.

The demand for greater convenience is born out of changes in working practices around the world. People are increasingly leading complex lives, with portfolio careers, second jobs, self-employment, and increased numbers of women at work. In the euro area, for instance, the number of people with second jobs went up by 25% in the decade to 2011. For busy people, the internet is a potential boon.

TIP: Focus on providing ultimate convenience in your online store and you will sell more.

Shoppers want to save time

One aspect of convenience has a special significance for online shoppers, and that is saving time. A study by Pew Internet, a lead-ing research group looking at the ways people use the web and internet technology, showed that 68% of people in the US believe that shopping online saves them time.[4]

However, as Paco Underhill, a pioneer of retail psychology, has shown, our perception of time is distorted in various ways when we are shopping.[5] Underhill's work looked at time factors in real-world, bricks-and-mortar stores, and one of its key findings was that we think we have spent less time in a store when we interact in some way. Considering that online stores often have a range of interactive capabilities – such as reviews or search systems – the chances are that our desire to save time is not matched by the amount of time we actually do spend in an online store. We end up searching around for a variety of things as well as reading reviews, for instance.

According to Alexa, a site that measures web activity, people spend around 16 minutes on eBay.co.uk each time they visit and look at an average of 17 pages in that time. That's just one shop, in one nation. In addition, most times we visit an online shop we do not actually buy anything; we go back repeatedly before we buy. The total time spent searching for, finding, and visiting alternative stores online can add up to more time being spent in total when we buy online than via traditional shopping.

Furthermore, a study by Marketing Charts showed that 50% of people spend three-quarters of their total online shopping time researching items that they later buy in bricks-and-mortar stores. In other words, people are adding time to their overall shopping activity by doing more research. Indeed, the study found that one in three people spend "a few days" conducting online research for products they intend buying in offline stores. That's hardly a timesaver, since in real-world stores we do not do anywhere near as much research and locating alternatives. Because that option is available to us online we take it up, but that can waste our time compared with shopping in bricks-and-mortar stores.

So why do people think that online shopping saves them time, when it often does the opposite? One of the reasons, as we have seen, is the distorting effect that the interactive nature of the web has on our perception of time. However, another factor is our emotional state. When we are involved in a highly focused, self-directed activity such as looking at things that interest us on websites, we tend to lose our concept of time and thus spend more time than we think.

Furthermore, there are other factors such as the light projected from the screen that can affect the levels of neurotransmitters in the brain, also altering how much attention we pay to time. The pineal gland, at the base of the brain, produces a hormone called melatonin, which has an effect on our sleep/wake rhythm. It is affected by the amount of light we receive and this in turn influences how awake we are. This has impacts on a range of psychological functions, including our sense of time passing. We may have been on a website for five minutes, but we could well think we have only been there for a minute or two.

TIP: Provide interactive features in your online store and people will think they are spending less time with you, thereby enhancing their view that they are saving time.

As a retailer, you don't want people to use your online shop too quickly in case they don't see what else is on offer, which does not help you increase your sales through upsells or cross-sells. Yet at the same time, online store owners need to make people think the system is fast, so that their perception of time passing is speedy, as the perception of saving time is a big draw. One way of achieving this is through the choice of color for the screen background, which has been shown to influence perception.[6] For instance, yellow tends to make people act more quickly on a website, whereas blue tends to slow them down. Choose the right screen color and your visitors could think that their shopping trip is going quickly; choose the wrong color and they may think that it is taking too much time.

Shoppers want low prices (sometimes)

Internet shoppers are also interesting in saving money. Due to the low infrastructure costs of web-based retail, an online store can be cheaper to set up than a traditional shop, and these savings can be passed on to shoppers. For example, online retailers do not need to spend money on creating dozens of beautiful and enticing bricks-and-mortar stores when all they require is one warehouse. They can employ fewer staff and their distribution costs may also be lower.

Many online retailers play on this cost-saving aspect. For example, in the US, home improvement store Lowes guarantees "everyday low prices" online, helping visitors focus on the very reason they want to shop on the web. In Australia and New Zealand, online department store OO has a guarantee that shoppers will pay the lowest price for anything: "we can offer amazing prices on an ever-increasing range of quality products and brands, so you can enjoy the thrill of getting exactly what you want at a bargain price." Similarly, the biggest online store in the Philippines, HalloHalloMall.com, focuses on deals, discounts, and giving its customers the best possible prices. In the UK, computer store PCWorld has several products with a "Web Only" price, showing a discount compared with buying the same item in the company's bricks-and-mortar stores.

However, low prices are not necessarily always what web shoppers are looking for. After all, if you wanted to buy a luxury yacht, would you really want the "bargain basement" version? Even though many surveys of online shopping point to the notion that buyers use the web to find bargains, this is only part of the story. Many people use online shops to buy from high-price, branded stores such as Gucci or McLaren. It therefore does not follow that if you run an online store you have to focus on offering low prices: it depends on what you are selling and to whom.

Interestingly, research suggests that people who have plenty of cash to spare, and could afford luxury brands, can be perfectly happy with lower-status items. The Chicago-based Beverage Testing Institute showed that Lithuanian vodka Gera, at $17.99 a liter, was top of a list of 75 brands on trial. Down toward the bottom of the list was Mystt, from the Colorado company Shadow Beverage, a premium spirit that at the time of testing was being sold for $75 a liter. Even though people may be attracted by premium brands, sometimes the cheaper version is perfectly adequate. This is because to be capable of realizing a high price, the premium brand needs to provide something else – social acceptance.

Shoppers want what other people buy

A powerful psychological factor in shopping is "social proof": we like to prove that we are part of "our group" or "our clan" by buying the same thing as everyone else in the group. It helps confirm our membership of the group and our acceptance as a member – the fact that we are liked. So, for instance, young mothers will want to choose the same kind of stroller as other young mothers in their town or neighborhood; teenage boys will want to buy their clothes from the same store as their friends, otherwise they will not feel accepted into their tribe. Amazon was one of the first online stores to realize this. At the bottom of each item on the site you can see "Customers who bought this item also bought" suggestions.

Social networks have a powerful role to play in this, because as we saw in the previous chapter, people can immediately share information on their purchases with their friends. And that's part of what makes the web so attractive to shoppers: it helps them ensure that they are buying the "right" things, the products and items that their group are buying.

Prior to internet shopping this was a much more cumbersome and comparatively slow process, so group members could often miss out on purchasing the right things. Now they can get up-to-the-minute information on what their group is buying, thereby making sure they can retain their membership and continue to be accepted.

Being part of a social group in this way also allows for competitive behavior to surface. People like to demonstrate that they have been first to the bargain, or were able to buy the very last item available. Social add-ons to online retail websites, such as a Twitter connection allowing people to send a tweet when they have bought something, are a good way of enabling this competitive spirit to surface. Similarly, a Facebook plugin that allows people to show that they "like" a product demonstrates to others what they have bought, helping them stand out among their friends.

TIP: Allow customers to display their competitive side with social media add-ons.

Academic research confirms that competitiveness is a key factor in our buying behavior.[7] Shoppers love getting the edge over another shopper. They want to be able to say that they managed to get an identical item but at a much lower price. Or they want to be able to say that theirs was delivered within hours of ordering, or perhaps that their purchase is so popular "no one has them any more – I managed to get the last one." Offline dinner parties (as well as online chat sites) are full of conversations in which people are making competitive boasts about their purchases.

CASE STUDY: KABOODLE

Kaboodle, started in 2007, is one of the original social shopping sites. It allows people to set up accounts where they create lists of items they have bought from a specific store or a style board of items that go together.

Around 70% of site visitors are female and most of the lists are about fashion, home, and style. Each user creates several style boards or lists depending on their personal preferences. Other people can then "follow" the individual, which means that as soon as they add something to their list or style board, their followers are immediately alerted to what has been bought. There is also the ability for interaction between users through a comment system.

According to Alexa, by mid-2013 Kaboodle was reaching only a quarter of the number of people it had in 2011. This suggests that even though it is a popular site, it is being taken over by other, more spontaneous ways of sharing purchases, such as Facebook and Twitter.

Shoppers want quick comparisons

One way consumers' competitiveness can find a home online is in the area of comparison shopping. Various websites compare prices, helping you find the best deal for your desired product. The idea behind these sites is that people are interested in getting the lowest prices; indeed, that's largely how they promote their services, showing consumers how they can save money. However, that's only one reason people like to use them.

Comparison sites are also proving so popular because they help people find products at a better price than other people – and they could perhaps increase their sales by ensuring they provide in addition a means of enabling people to buy competitively, such as by showing lists of friends who have just bought something via the site. And if you don't think competitive buying exists, you haven't heard of eBay.

Shoppers want choice

According to *The Guinness World Records*, the largest bookstore in the world is run by Barnes & Noble in New York. It has almost 13 miles of shelving, enough to hold about 249,600 books. The problem for Barnes & Noble is that in America alone, 328,000 new books are published each year. Indeed, if it wanted to fit in all the books available, it would have to increase the size of its store by 520 times.

The result is that most books are not available on the shelves, even though it's the biggest store of its kind in the world.

The problem is repeated in every kind of bricks-and-mortar store. There simply is not the physical space in a fashion shop to show every kind of dress, in every size; nor is it possible for shoe shops to stock or display every shoe that is made (although Selfridges' men's shoe department in London has a good go, stocking over 250 brands). Whatever kind of real-world shop you consider, what it offers is a limited range. We are given only the illusion of choice.

Online, however, we can get the full range. The world's biggest online store is Alibaba, a Chinese company that sells almost everything anyone could ever want. Indeed, its total sales exceed those of Amazon and eBay combined. It achieves this with a massive range of items in all kinds of categories, all easily available via a comprehensive search engine.

Even if a shopper does not use Alibaba, a search engine can more than likely find them what they want among the thousands of web pages. In other words, the internet provides consumers with real choice.

So for centuries, retailers have only been able to concentrate on providing the top items, the ones that sell the most. Pop into any large supermarket and you will find the Top 100 CDs on sale or the Top 100 DVDs, out of the millions that are actually available. The shelf space is competing for many other products.

The music identification service Shazam has indexed more than 27 million tracks to which people have listened. Or take Gracenote, part of the Sony Corporation, which has over 130 million music tracks in its database. That's enough for around 13 million albums. And the Gracenote index only deals with the music that people play. Some of the music gets significant attention – the Top 100, for instance – but the 130 millionth track? That may only be played a couple of times a year.

This is a real issue for retailers: some products are wanted, but only by a couple of people in the world. If you stock those products in your Chicago store and the potential buyers are in Adelaide, you have missed out on sales. The fewer buyers there are for a product, the greater the logistics issues become. This is a

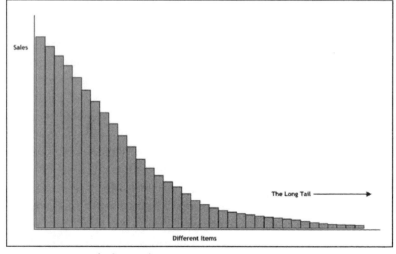

Figure 1   The long tail

concept known as the "long tail," which is well known in business and was popularized by former *Wired* journalist Chris Anderson.

If you look at a typical "long tail" bar chart of product sales (Figure 1), you can see that most of the sales are in the initial portion of the chart – the head. For items that are less popular, clearly the bars on the chart are smaller. However, when you add all the bars in the long tail together (Figure 2), they represent more sales than the top items.

This means two things. If retailers could somehow solve their logistics problems and their shelf space issues, they would make more money from the cumulative total of the long tail than from the popular items. Secondly, the long tail represents true choice. People can buy what they want, rather than being forced to buy the popular items or having little choice.

Buyers like to feel in control: they prefer to choose what they want, not what the retailer decides to sell them. Bricks-and-mortar retailers like to claim that they stock a wide range, but as is obvious from these examples, such retailers offer only an illusion of choice because of storage and logistics limitations.

However, the internet solves both the choice issue for shoppers and the logistics and storage issues for retailers. It doesn't

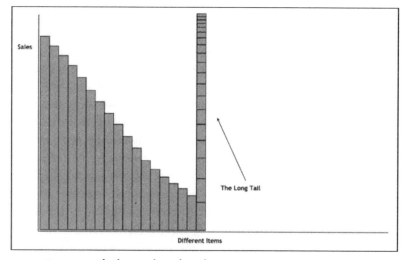

Figure 2   The long tail combined

matter where those long-tail buyers might be in the world, they can
find a website to sell them exactly what they choose to purchase.
Equally, for retailers who want to offer a huge range, it doesn't
matter that they cannot stock everything, because they can sell anything on their website and source it from the original suppliers. The
result is that shoppers flock to the internet instead of real-world
stores because they can control what they want to buy and exercise
real choice – a key element of convenience.

Shoppers want easy availability

The concept of the long tail is not only about choice, it is also about
availability, another crucial reason for shopping online – whatever
people want is likely to be available somewhere. Instead of having
to wait for things from bricks-and-mortar stores that may have to
order an item in, online shoppers can find who has what they want
in stock, right now.

Indeed, researching his doctoral thesis at Erasmus University,
Rotterdam, Laurens Sloot discovered that lack of availability of products in (offline) supermarkets was a significant cause of annoyance for

shoppers.[8] Online, this frustration can largely be eliminated, because if one shop does not have something a shopper can try another store within a second or two: availability is only a click away.

Nevertheless, most traditional retailers are not focusing on this key aspect of online shopping. Instead, many are far too busy trying to replicate their offline stores, thereby not demonstrating the breadth and depth of choice available and making visitors think that the online store is a replica of the offline shop with which they are already frustrated. For instance, bricks-and-mortar stores often do not show products in categories, but in related displays. A department store might have a bedroom display selling the furniture, the linen, the curtains, and the accessories all in the same place. Online, people are searching mostly for something specific, and want to see and compare all the bedside lights, for example, alongside one another. However, there can be instances where both approaches work.

CASE STUDY: MARISOTA

Marisota is an online fashion store run by direct selling company J.D. Williams. The website is aimed mainly at women who are above size 12, so it retails predominantly so-called plus sizes for larger women, although it does cater for men as well. The website is very popular, ranked at around 3,000 in the UK by Alexa. One of the reasons for its popularity is that few fashion stores on the High Street provide much beyond "average" sizes. In addition, there is the added embarrassment of having to ask for a large size, only to find that you are too big for that store. Shopping online for larger sizes is more convenient and less embarrassing and Marisota makes it easy for women to do this.

The site is broken down into traditional fashion categories, such as coats, dresses, tops, lingerie, hats, and gloves. However, it has also taken a leaf out of offline retail's book by providing themes, such as "mother of the bride," "cruisewear," and "workwear," which bring together a range of items from different categories into one mini-shop that allows shoppers to see clothes that they might want to buy

> as part of an ensemble, so they don't have to jump from cat-
> egory to category to find what they want.

Getting what you want straight away is of course a key aspect of availability. This did not start with the internet, however.

In the early nineteenth century, going into a store involved waiting in line to be served by a "counter assistant." He or she would take your order and collect all the items you wanted. Either you would have to wait in the store until they had obtained everything on your list, or they would get it delivered to your home later on. Indeed, as a small child in Britain in the early 1960s I remember going into our village Co-operative store with my mother. She would hand in her list, get a bill, and then walk over to a woman who sat in the middle of the shop in a kind of glass cupboard, where she paid. Then we would walk out of the shop and go home, without any shopping. The next day, a young man would turn up at our house on a bicycle that had a huge wicker basket on the front, in which would be our shopping in a box, which he would bring into our kitchen.

It was Clarence Saunders, founder of the self-service shop Piggly Wiggly in Memphis, Tennessee in 1916, who was the first to allow customers to select the items they wanted and pay at a central cash desk.[9] Supermarkets were initially popularized in America in the 1930s and spread to the UK in the 1950s. However, the notion of self-service shopping did not really start to spread around the globe until the 1990s; now the developing world has seen a signifi-cant surge in self-service shops because they appeal to people. But why? After all, we are doing the work. The shop owner simply has to stock the shelves, sit at the cash desk, and take the money. We select the items, push them around the store in a shopping cart, or carry a basket, and then once we have paid for our items, we pack them into bags ourselves and transport them home. Prior to supermarkets, the shop assistants did all that for us.

The real reason we like self-service shopping is because we can get what we want, when we want it, which is usually *now*. The attraction is availability: when we want to buy something, we don't like having to wait longer than necessary to get it. But even here there are nuances.

A classic study of waiting times, conducted in Switzerland in 1994, compared how people reacted to waiting in line at the post office with their feelings about waiting in Migros, a popular superstore. It showed that people disliked waiting at the post office, but were more prepared to accept waiting in line at the supermarket.[10] While the study really focused on how waiting time affected a shopper's mood, it did highlight that when people know exactly what they want – from a very limited selection of goods – they want it even faster, with no waiting.

Interestingly, online supermarkets are almost returning us to the days before self-service: they take our shopping list from us and then deliver all our groceries in boxes. While delivery may not be as instantaneous as collecting the goods ourselves, we can arrange a slot of an hour or two that is convenient and fits in with the rest of our activities.

Shoppers want delivery on their terms

In fact, delivery options for most online stores tend to be much more based around the requirements of the customer than at bricks-and-mortar retailers. One of the issues with real-world shops is that you can only take the items away with you that they have in stock. If the store needs to order something, you have to go back and collect it. Alternatively, if you order a sizable item that needs to be delivered, such as a fridge, you are told when delivery will take place, without having much choice about the timing, and indeed you may be given a delivery window as wide as half a day or even more.

It is often very different with online retailers. At Amazon UK, for instance, there is the choice of next-day delivery or delivery over several days, either to your home or another nominated address. You can also choose to have your item delivered to an Amazon Locker, a secure box in an area such as a filling station or tube station, where you can collect it at your convenience and often with 24-hour availability. Instead of being forced to wait at home for a parcel, or having to collect it from the delivery firm if it tried to deliver when you were out, you can get the item when you want from where you want. Online fashion store Asos provides similar flexibility by collaborating with delivery company Collect+, which offers thousands of collection points in local stores and also deals with returns to major online retailers.[11] eBay offers same-day delivery in some regions, as does Walmart.

Such developments ensure that those who shop online are in control of when and where they get their items, and they are becoming used to online orders being customized to their terms, something that traditional retailers find difficult to match.

BLUEPRINT

People are attracted to online shopping for some rather basic motivations. If your online store appeals to these factors, then you will have the basis for a good shop.

1. Emphasize convenience. Make sure that products are easy to find and that delivery is as fast as possible.
2. Make sure that your online shop works quickly, or at least that people perceive it to work quickly.
3. Only show low prices when you know this is what people are really looking for. Price is not always the issue for a consumer.
4. Shoppers buy things their friends buy, so social activities should feature highly in your online store.
5. Appeal to shoppers' competitive nature by allowing them to show off when they get a deal.
6. Provide the maximum possible amount of choice.
7. Ensure you have a wide range of delivery options so that people can get items they have bought on their terms, when and where they want.

3
HOW PEOPLE SHOP ONLINE

When I wrote *Travel and Holidays on the Internet* in 1999, I told the story of my first ever foray into online shopping:

On 12th April 1994 I arrived rather cautiously at the reception desk of the Hotel Metropole in central Geneva, just opposite the famous lake. I was a little worried because I had not spoken to anyone to book the room. Instead, I had used an American hotel booking service that had just been launched on CompuServe. I was concerned that my electronic search for a room would have been fruitless, but I was keen to see whether the system worked. Thankfully, it had, and I was able to spend a couple of nights in the comfort of room 203.

This was my first venture into online travel booking and since then I have seen a revolution in the way such facilities work. Just over five years ago, there were only online services like CompuServe, America On Line and Dialog. Since then, these individual networks have been subsumed by the Internet which has provided even greater travel options than was thought possible just a few years ago.

Back in 1994, the hotel booking service was a text only service that looked like a black and white version of Teletext. It was extraordinarily slow, compared with today's booking systems, but it was remarkable even then. You could ask the CompuServe system to locate available rooms in hotels anywhere in the world. Of course, the system did not search every hotel, instead it only used hotels that had registered for the service. Even so, you could enter a city name, a star rating for your hotel and within a few minutes, you'd have a list of available spaces. You then had to select the one you wanted and give some details of your intended stay, before a price was returned to your screen. If this was acceptable, you could make a booking. Your only confirmation of your reservation was your

printout (if you had remembered to do one!) of this final screen. Yet
it was exciting; you no longer had to trek into town, visit a few
travel agents and laboriously go through pages of hotel listings.
You then had to get the agent to call the hotels, struggle through
language barriers only to discover the place was full on the night
you wanted. Back to square one! Using the CompuServe system
was so much easier – and even though the on-line transaction
took about 20 minutes, it was still much faster than going off to a
travel agent.[1]

You can tell I was somewhat excited and impressed, but looking back
at that now it all seems so primitive. If a hotel-booking website took
20 minutes today, we'd be waving goodbye to it. However, when I
took those pioneering steps I could only select rooms from a tiny
number of available hotels that had signed up to CompuServe. Plus,
if I wanted information about the room (whether it had an ensuite
bathroom, for instance) I could not get it; I had to phone, or visit the
library to thumb through an international directory of hotels, which
could well have been printed a year or two earlier. I would have
needed to do this so I was sure I booked the correct thing.

Shoppers are information seekers

When we buy something, we like to make sure we are buying the
right item. We don't like mystery or being made a fool of. Neither
do we like the hassle of having to return products if they are not
quite what we expected. Prior to the internet, sales assistants in
traditional retailers would spend time with you and answer your
questions; now the best online stores have information pages that
perform a similar function.

In an Australian study of information seeking among consumers, researchers at the University of Queensland looked at how
car buyers behaved before they made their decision to buy.[2] The
study was conducted in 1981, before the invention of the World
Wide Web, but its conclusions about behavior are still valid. The
researchers classified shoppers into three kinds: those who do not

do much information seeking when buying a car, those who seek a lot of information, and those who are selective about the kind of information they are looking for. The study also confirmed earlier work showing that this kind of classification was actually quite tricky. It transpires that a combination of factors, including personality type, time pressures, perceived costs of search, and previous brand experience, all influence each other to determine the extent to which customers seek out new information about the products they are buying.

What we can definitively say, however, is that consumers are information seekers. Some might look for more or less information than others, but people want to get as much information as they need to help them make an informed decision about their purchases. With the wide availability of information on the internet, including reviews from fellow consumers, clearly people are more than able to satisfy their thirst for product information.

Yet this conflicts with the requirements of the seller. As Donald Case explains in his book *Looking for Information*:

> From the marketer's perspective, the information that is put out in print, on radio and television, on the Internet and on billboards would result ideally in an entirely knee-jerk reaction: the consumer sees the ads, then sees the product, and then buys the product. For those who make and sell products, it is better that the consumer does not engage in a lengthy search for information, but simply buys the item as quickly as possible.[3]

The breadth and depth of information available online mean that there is no shortage for the consumer who wants to be well informed, whether the marketer wants that or not.

In their annual report on the world's top retail brands, analysts Interbrand said, "Today's consumers spend significantly more time in the research phase, considering an ever-expanding array of brands before making a choice."[4] The report added, "Such changes to consumers' decision processes mean that traditional strategies used by retail marketers will no longer work." In other words, if you run a shop online you are going to have to do things differently in order to succeed. Online retailers need to see themselves much more as publishers of information and much less as shops.

> TIP: Pack your website with information about your products and services – not only brief details, but as many pages as possible with background information, usage information, and so on, so customers can find information relevant to their needs.

You can see many online retailers grasping this concept. In Australia, for instance, leading supermarket chain Woolworths has a large number of pages of information and useful content – none of which actually sells a product directly. For example, there is a "Kids' Site" within the Health & Wellbeing section that features coloring-in activities as well as a lunchbox planner and educational articles, such as "Where does food come from?" Over at the Fresh Food Inspiration section you can "Meet Our Growers" to find out information about how the foodstuffs Woolworths sells in its online store are produced.

Similarly, US-based global food manufacturer General Mills, which owns brands such as "Cheerios" in the UK and "Yoki" in Brazil, has a website with background information on all its products as well as useful additional material such as recipes and nutritional data. Before you even venture into the online store or down to your local supermarket, this website can furnish you with plenty of detailed information about the products you might want to buy.

German pharmacy chain DM's website is exclusively information based and is rich with features about health issues and product details. If you want to buy anything, you have to head over to Amazon, where the company has its own branded shop.

Belgian fashion store Honestby.com takes information provision to an extreme level, offering every last detail about the items on sale. It shows the carbon footprint of each product as well as details of the suppliers and costs of each element of the product. The company claims that it is the first 100% transparent business. Not only that, its website includes extensive news about the world of fashion in general.

The information-seeking shopper is looking for details. They want to know all about the product or service they are thinking of buying. They want to know its history, how it is used, and the kind of people who use it, and they want access to manuals and technical details. They also want to be able to read reviews and see what other people think of an item. Furthermore, they want to see the product being used in videos or hear it discussed in audio podcasts. Overall, they want as much information as they can lay their hands on to help them be certain they are going to buy the right thing.

Nevertheless, not all customers are information seekers. Some are quick buyers, who do not want all this extra information. They prefer to see a picture of the item and a short description confirming that it is what they want, together with the price, the shipping and tax information, and a "buy now" button.

For example, the online store Shop Clues is a Top 100 website in India. The website receives a large number of visitors and has proved to be a major success since it began in 2011. However, it is clearly a site for people who already know what they want – it is not targeting those who are searching for information. There is a central search box to find the specific item you desire, as well as clearly labeled departments for different kinds of items. The design is not geared to browsing but to going direct to a particular type of product.

> TIP: Decide which kind of shopper you want to aim at – the information seeker or the quick buyer – and design your website accordingly.

How shoppers gather information

For a moment, just imagine you are watching a woman in her 40s sitting in her lounge with a laptop on her lap, intent on buying a new dress for an important occasion in a few weeks' time. Let's call her Liz. She knows the style of dress she wants and the color she is looking for. But she isn't sure where to get it from: her usual online fashion store doesn't deal in this "occasion" kind of dress, so she has to start in a search engine.

What Liz gets in terms of results will very much depend on what she types in, of course. But let's assume she is an experienced web user who enters more than merely the word "dresses." If she types something like "dresses for special occasions," she will first be presented with several shops. Google assumes that when people search for something specific like this they are in buying or "transactional" mode. However, this is a false assumption, and in my informal studies of web users it is an assumption that is a frequent source of annoyance. When people are in information-seeking mode they do not want to be presented with web content that is designed to sell them something.

Indeed, research from Pennsylvania State University shows that 90% of searches are informational or navigational – looking for a specific site – and only 10% are transactional.[5] For instance, if someone types "happylittlesoles" into Google, the search engine acts rather like a telephone directory, taking them to where they want to go, the information-based Happy Little Soles children's shoe shop.

By focusing on transactional searches, Google is making life more difficult for Liz. Clicking on the first search result takes her to a "buy now" page, which annoys her because even though she does want to buy a dress, at the moment she merely wants information on the suitability of her idea. So she goes back to Google and clicks on another link.

This is a common feature in search behavior. Even though 53% of people click on the first result,[6] many of them also click on subsequent results or return to search again because the pages presented to them were not what they wanted. In a mathematical analysis of search behavior, researchers from the University of Washington, Seattle and Microsoft found that there is an 80% chance of people looking at additional search results within 10 seconds of being given the first potential answer to their query.[7] They then perform a range of search adaptations, with an 80% chance that five minutes after their original search they will specialize their search request, adding more details to focus in on what they want.

Liz continues just like this, going back and forth between Google's search results and the pages it presents to her. It is familiar territory to us all. Partly, of course, it is our fault for not thinking through the precise wording of our search, or not using the "Advanced Search" facility, which would allow us to narrow down our results, for example by region, how recently an item was published, or whether specific languages are used.

The problem is that many shoppers like Liz appear to think that Google is psychic. As a result, Liz takes longer than she hoped to find out the information she wants. This frustration with search results can lead her to think less favorably toward the companies from which she might eventually buy. Researchers in America found that frustration with search engine results could lead to a lower intention to purchase under some circumstances, such as when the search interrupts "flow" by providing results that are not consistent with expectations.[8] This suggests that if companies do not provide information that searchers want and make sure that information is easily reachable, then lower sales are likely.

To provide that information you first need to know what people are already searching for in relation to what you sell. For instance, you might call the item you sell "ABC123," but your shoppers might use something much vaguer and so be unable to locate your item quickly. Keyword research tools such as that provided in Google AdWords – the advertising system run by Google – are a good way of finding out what terms you need to include in your web pages to attract hits quickly.

> TIP: Make sure that your product information can be found easily by search engines so that you reduce the chances of frustration for searchers and thereby enhance the likelihood of successful sales.

Liz gives up with Google and decides instead to visit some trusted brands she already knows, in the hope that they will have information about "dresses for occasions" on their websites. The biggest brand most people know is Amazon, which is the second most popular search tool for information on products after Google. Brands that incorporate extensive information about products on their websites and link back to that from other websites such as YouTube tend to serve people like Liz well because they are easily findable. This is important because, as Interbrand said in its 2012 Report, "With the rapid adoption of technology, it's the consumers who are out in front, not the industry."

Shopping technology is changing

There has been an exponential rise in shopping using mobile devices, such as smartphones or tablets, including the Apple iPad and Google Nexus. According to consultancy firm IDC Financial Insights, the number of people buying products and services directly from their mobile doubled in just one year, 2011. Similarly, according to Shop.org, a community for digital retailers, the rise in mobile use is continuing at a rapid pace. According to its 2012 Social and Mobile Consumer Study, the number of people buying from mobile devices in the US trebled from the end of 2010 to the end of 2011. This combined with a surge in the ownership of smartphones – in Korea, for instance, 59% of all mobile phones in use are smartphones. In the UK, it is predicted that smartphone penetration will grow to almost 72% of mobile phone usage in 2015, compared with a 53% penetration for the US. Furthermore, technology consultancy Gartner claims that mobiles will soon be more prevalent than computers as a means of connecting to the internet. Wherever you look for statistics about the uptake of mobile devices, the data always look the same – massive rises in numbers with steeply climbing graphs.

As Chuck Martin says in his book *The Third Screen*, mobile shopping will "forever change the company–customer interaction." He adds that the increase in mobile uptake will mean that even in bricks-and-mortar stores, there is a completely different way ahead for interacting with mobile-using customers.[9] Shoppers will be able to buy what they want, when they want it, rather than having to remember it and shop later, when they get home – or perhaps forget what they wanted in the first place because the "moment" has passed. Partly, Martin explains, the considerable computing power within the smartphone allows users to get highly specific, location-based information that will help them save time and money because they will be able to see what can be bought around them, there and then. For instance, a smartphone could detect a nearby florist, know from its calendar that it is the phone owner's wife's birthday in a day or two, and suggest he pop in and order some flowers, giving driving or walking directions to the relevant shop.

CASE STUDY: MEAT PACK

Meat Pack is a shoe store chain in Guatemala, Central America. It used mobiles and location-based campaigns very effectively in a campaign to "steal" customers from rival stores, such as Nike. When a user of the Meat Pack smartphone app entered a rival shoe store, the app knew where the individual was, thanks to location-based positioning using GPS on the phone. So up popped an alert on the phone pointing out that Meat Pack offered shoes at a discount price compared with the store where the individual was shopping. The discount initially offered was massive – a 99% price reduction. But it was reduced by 1% for every second, giving people just over a minute and a half to run down the street to the nearby Meat Pack store and grab a bargain. In one week alone, Meat Pack gained 600 new shoppers this way, giving one lucky shopper an 89% discount on some trainers because they had managed to get to the shop in ten seconds.

Mobile capability is no longer a "nice to have" for an online shop, it is an essential. I made this very statement at a 2013 workshop for marketing executives in Estonia, where I was challenged about it. One of the delegates suggested that this might well be true for technology-based nations such as America, Japan, or much of Europe, but what about developing nations such as Africa or parts of Asia? I was able to point out that the world's largest and – so far – most successful mobile payment system is M-pesa, which started in Kenya and is now available in several other countries, including Tanzania and India. It allows people with mobile phones to spend money as though they had the cash in their pockets. As the *Guardian* newspaper pointed out toward the end of 2012, Africa is becoming a mobile-centric continent, with whole nations essentially skipping out on desktop computers and going directly to mobile. If anything, mobile commerce is therefore more important in developing nations than in the developed world.

Consider for a moment life in a village in a remote part of Africa before the mobile phone. Getting goods, services, and money was a difficult and cumbersome task. The nearest bank might be a day away, or more; the distances in Africa are significant and commerce, shopping, logistics, and general business are all difficult and expensive to operate. However, with the mobile phone, many of the problems associated with distance are eliminated. What is more, endemic problems such as lack of electricity to charge mobile batteries are being overcome by innovative companies such as Fenix International, which is creating cost-effective mobile phone charging systems powered by the sun. African news website AllAfrica reports that by 2015 more people in Africa will have access to a mobile phone network than to electricity. In other words, to suggest that mobile shopping is only something that takes place in high-tech countries is to misunderstand that mobile is fast creating shopping opportunities across the globe.

Mobile will soon become the main way people connect with online stores.

People do not necessarily buy directly on their smartphones – typically they use their mobile devices to find information about prices or where stock might be available. They may also want to take pictures of potential purchases, as a means of checking details later or to share with their friends. The mobile device is also used to look up reviews of items that shoppers have seen in a bricks-and-mortar store.

TIP: Have free wi-fi in your bricks-and-mortar stores because it encourages use of the web on mobile devices, helping people feel more informed and more likely to buy from you.

Mobile shoppers treat stores as showrooms

The whole issue of "showrooming" is another aspect of mobile technology to which many offline retailers have been slow to adapt. Showrooming takes place when people visit a bricks-and-mortar store but then buy online, using a smartphone or tablet, thus treating the real-world shop as nothing more than a showroom. They may do this because they can get an online discount, or to have the item delivered so they don't have to carry it home. Their first preference is to visit the online shop of the store in which they are actually standing, although research in Canada has shown that this is not always the case. The study found that people would buy in a competitor's online shop if they would get even a small discount.[10] It also demonstrated that the discount does not have to be substantial: as little as 2.5% off the in-store price would get people buying online.

 Some bricks-and-mortar retailers have realized that people are using their stores as showrooms and have added QR codes to the items on display in their shops. These codes, like the one on the left, take people to a specific web page when they point their smartphone at them. QR means "Quick Response" and around 14 million people a month in the US alone scan such codes. This one takes you to the web page for this book at Click.ology.biz.

In South Korea, QR codes are used extensively by supermarket chain Tesco in its "virtual" stores.[11] These are "shops" that appear at traditional poster sites, such as at bus stops and in the subway in Seoul. The electronic displays provide a visual copy of a real-world store – it looks as though you are standing in an aisle of a supermarket, facing the shelves. While waiting for the bus, people can do their shopping by scanning the QR codes of the items they want to buy, which will then be delivered later to their home.

While other retailers are experimenting with such systems, including Walmart in the US, the use of QR codes is not yet widespread. A study in Boston found that in 700 bricks-and-mortar shops surveyed in the US, only 7% used them.[12] Most of these codes were aimed at young people and were to be found in high-tech stores; mainstream shops were not exploiting the opportunity.

At the beginning of 2013, I queried the low uptake of QR codes with a real-world retail customer of mine. "Why don't your 120 stores use QR codes?" I asked.

"Because it will encourage people to buy off the website," my client replied.

"That's rather the point," I said, "it gets people to buy your products."

However, my client pointed out that QR codes pose a management problem for many bricks-and-mortar retailers. Sales staff often work on commission; if someone is showrooming and scans in a QR code, then leaves the store to buy online, the staff in the store are denied the opportunity for that payment. Even if retail staff are not on commission, a bricks-and-mortar store needs to sell the products it has on display because of stock and logistics issues. Thus showrooming, encouraged by QR codes, only complicates matters for such retailers.

The real issue is perhaps the conservative approach of many retailers, who find it difficult to innovate. Rather than QR codes being the problem, lack of willingness to change staff structures, remuneration systems, and store processes is more of a barrier. My client did not want to introduce QR codes because it would mean the kind of staff his company employs would not be appropriate – it would need to employ people who were much better informed about products, because showrooming customers turn to store staff as an information resource, a walking encyclopedia, which is a different skill from selling. Many shops are also unionized, meaning that any changes to working practices need the agreement of unions before they can be put in place.

Nevertheless, some traditional industries are taking up QR codes, such as the funeral business. In Shanghai, a QR code can be put on the gravestone of a loved one so that people can scan it and visit a tribute-style website celebrating the individual's life. This can also be done in the US, Japan, and the UK. It doesn't require much of a change to operating practice and can generate additional income through charging for such an extra service.

CASE STUDY: YEBHI.COM

Yebhi.com is a leading online department store in India. The company was launched in 2009 and has proved immensely popular for clothing, shoes, and household items. It now has 30 real-world stores in coffee shops in Delhi and Bangalore, but even so, you can't actually get hold of the products on display. The system works like this. A wall of the coffee shop has poster displays of popular products. Each item on show has a QR code beside it, meaning that people can sip their coffee and shop at the same time. Not only that, when they do this the system provides them with a discount code for their next cup of coffee.

This is an indication that where smartphones are popular, as in India, QR codes have a place to play in furthering business for online stores, by combining them with a real-world activity. This taps into the psychology of convenience. Not only is it convenient to shop while drinking coffee, the QR code takes the shopper directly to the order page for that individual product. This is even more convenient than going to the website and then having to search or select from various menu options.

Despite potential difficulties in their implementation, QR codes do represent an opportunity for bricks-and-mortar retailers. For instance, imagine you run a retailer selling mid-price fashion items. You place a QR code on the tags, which a customer could then scan using their mobile phone. This would lead to a web page being shown on their phone where they could either gain more information about the item, or buy it directly online. The problem is that you would be holding stock in the store that you need to shift, which would not be sold if the potential buyer went to the online store. But what if the QR code took them instead to a simple web page that fitted entirely into the screen of their mobile device? It would not scroll: all it would have on it would be a number and the words "Show this

discount voucher at the checkout and get 2.5% off." This would be
enough to entice them to buy, and by using the QR code in this way
you would have gained rather than lost the customer.

> TIP: QR codes can be employed in a variety of ways. By think-
> ing about how you can apply them creatively, you can gain
> customers and sell products.

If you only have an online shop, with no real-world presence, giving
people QR codes when they are already on your website would be
a waste of time and effort. So online-only retailers need to be innovative to benefit from the use of QR codes. For example, a QR code
on packaging could take a customer directly to information about the
product they have just bought, or to a customer service web page, a
social media page, or a review site. That's before you consider the use
of such devices in advertising, when advertisers can include a QR code
in a printed advertisement or on a poster, which leads people to further information about the specific product or service the advert is for.

> The advantage of QR codes is that you can direct people to
> precise and specific web locations that are designed with par-
> ticular aims in mind. That means you can control the pathway
> taken by the customer much more easily.

People want one of two things when they use the internet for shopping: they either want information on products and services – lots
of it – or they want to do something specific, such as buy an item
or get a voucher. They want to do this quickly, because the internet
provides so many other distractions to pursue. QR codes are one
way of dealing with this growing problem for retailers: the reduction in consumers' attention spans.

Shoppers have low attention spans

The time for which we are prepared to devote our attention to
something appears to be lower now than it has been for decades.

Indeed, according to the website Statistic Brain, human beings currently have an attention span that is less than that of a goldfish. The site suggests that even in 2008 we had a much longer attention span, 12 seconds compared with just 8 seconds today. However, for online retailers the picture is worse. A study in 2006 found that people stop paying attention in online stores after a mere 4 seconds.[13] Whichever statistics you look at, though, we clearly live in a world where people are rapidly chopping and changing from one website to another and gathering material from a wide array of places, all within a relatively short timeframe. We simply cannot pay attention to everything to the same degree – there simply is not enough time.

The result of this reduction in attention span means that we are spending much less time on a website now than ever before. People are quick to leave a web page if they cannot immediately see what they want, so online retailers need to provide sharply focused and easy-to-use navigation; this will also demonstrate to customers that they are "liked," because the website has been focused on their needs. eBay and Asos are two leading retail sites that share a common simple feature – a central search box. This means that even someone with a very short attention span can land on the page and quickly get to where they want to go by searching for it.

> TIP: To make your online store more successful, invest in a thorough search facility so that visitors can find anything straightaway. This appeals to those with low attention spans.

Psychologically, the term "attention span" is rather broad; indeed, there are plenty of separate attention spans:

◆ *Visual attention span*: how much attention our eyes pay to certain features we see on a website.
◆ *Conscious attention span*: the amount of time we give something before making a decision or becoming bored and wanting to move on.

◆ *Subconscious attention span*: a hidden decision-making process of which we are not aware, but which triggers us to stop looking at something, reading it, or even thinking about it.

Internet retailers need to account for these different kinds of attention spans if they are to succeed in capturing and maintaining our attention.

Shoppers move their eyes a lot

Eye-tracking technology can help retailers understand what people are looking at on a web page and for how long. The most common means of checking how our eyes move when we look at a web page is to have a specially adapted computer screen that projects infrared light toward the user. This is reflected into video cameras around the screen, which can then track the reflection from the center of the eye over the pupil.[14] The resulting analysis of the videos shows that our eyes do not travel in a linear fashion but move in a variable way, often jumping around and not even looking at the whole page in front of us.

You don't realize you are doing this, but observe someone as they are reading something and watch their eyes. They don't move in a straight line across the text but instead jump up and down. Whether you are looking at a page of printed text or a computer screen, your eyes have short periods where they stay on a point, called a fixation, and then sudden, jerky, up-and-down movements called saccades. According to Robert Crowder and Richard Wagner in *The Psychology of Reading*, our eye movements are "ballistic."[15] By this they mean that the sudden and dramatic movements of our eyes are rather like bullets: once they set off in a direction, they do so rapidly and in a straight line without the ability to change direction until that movement stops. Furthermore, when your eyes are in their saccadic phase, jumping up from the item you are looking at, visual signals to the brain are suppressed. You are temporarily blind for fractions of seconds as you look at a web page.

In a novel series of experiments in the late 1990s at the University of Illinois, researcher John Grimes showed that people were unable to notice changes to images when those changes happened during a saccade.[16] Participants looked at images of two men wearing different hats. In one image, the man on the left had a light-colored hat and the man on the right had a dark-colored hat. The second image was identical, except that the hats had been swapped using photo-editing software, with the light-colored hat now on the right. The pictures were shown to people on a computer, which flashed the swapped picture during the jerky eye movements. There were also other image-manipulation tests, such as someone wearing a pink swimsuit that was changed to green, and a scene showing a crowd of 30 puffins, 10 of which were removed for the second picture. Whatever the image manipulation, people could not spot the change if the pictures were presented during saccades, even if they were told in advance that they would see alterations. This is known in popular psychology as "change blindness"[17] and could be important for online retailers, who often use flashing or moving images to gain attention. If those flashes happen when people are jerking their eyes, they will not see them – they are invisible.

However, our jerky eye movements also give us a gap in which to move our gaze. That means that we might not land back at exactly the same spot on the screen. Eye-tracking research shows that as well as our eyes jumping up and down, we also zigzag around a web page. In essence, this means that we look only fleetingly at what is on a web page. Combined with subconscious decisions about whether or not we like what we see, change blindness, and the conscious decision to move quickly on to the next thing because of our busy lives, this all adds up to shoppers who don't see things in the way you might want them to online.

For example, studies by web usability expert Jakob Nielsen have shown that 69% of a viewer's time on a web page is spent looking at the left-hand side.[18] Furthermore, only 20% of people pay attention to items when they are below the bottom of the screen and they have to scroll down to look at them.[19] If you design your web pages with items that you want shoppers to see on the right or "below the fold," you are seriously reducing your potential sales.

TIP: Focus your most important content on the top left of
the screen, if your visitors read from left to right. If they read
from right to left, put your most important content at the top
right.

Usability research does miss out an important factor – the subconscious processing that happens when we look at a web page. Other
research shows that even though we are not consciously aware of
material in our peripheral vision, we do process it. Importantly,
neurological studies demonstrate that information from our
peripheral vision can go directly to our emotional centers and the
decision-making parts of our brain.[20]

In other words, people are making emotional decisions about
whether or not they like your website based on information reaching their brain of which they are not even aware. This means
that if you have material on the edges of your page that people
generally dislike – such as garish pictures – they may not be consciously aware of them, but these items will be helping them form
an impression of your site. It could influence their emotional reaction toward you, your products, and your services. Equally, if there
is something broken on your site, such as a missing image, it may
not be a problem in how they navigate the site, except that if people
see it in their peripheral vision they will probably think less of you.
Alternatively, of course, you can ensure that you position material
in the "cold" peripheral vision of your website visitors that elicits a
positive reaction: close-ups of relevant faces, such as typical buyers,
often produce a warm, positive subconscious reaction.

It is probably a good idea to get some eye-tracking research
done on your website. Not only will this help you understand what
people are looking at, and what in your design works well, it will
also show you what people are not looking at, and what is in a visitor's peripheral vision. If you cannot afford eye-tracking research,
the next best option is to track mouse movement and clicking
behavior, which you can study yourself using something like Crazy
Egg or Clicktale. These programs follow a website visitor around
the page, constantly monitoring what is displayed on their screen,
where their mouse moves, and what they click on.

Remember too that eye movement on mobile devices such as tablets will be different from on a standard computer screen, and will vary in portrait and in landscape mode. For example, if someone holds their smartphone in landscape mode they can see less depth of information, but if they hold it in portrait mode they can't see wide items such as images. If portions of your page are cut off because the screen isn't wide enough or information is missing because the screen isn't long enough, people get frustrated because they have to scroll around or move the page to see things. Furthermore, on a tablet device people expect to flick or swipe from side to side and not scroll downward, whereas on a desktop or a smartphone, those same pages need to scroll from top to bottom. Younger users, more experienced in touch devices, will expect much more of your page to respond to touch commands, whereas older visitors, used to the earlier incarnations of the web, will be looking for "click here" buttons. This means you can no longer have one kind of web page that is delivered to everyone – you need specific designs and functions for each kind of device people might use.

Shoppers find online stores difficult to use

Designing a bricks-and-mortar store is relatively straightforward. People enter through the main door and can see items on the shelves ahead of and around them. There are aisles taking them in a clearly defined route around those shelves, and there is an obvious place to pay. Also, most shops are much like the ones next door, apart from the general styling and the goods on sale.

Online, however, retailers often present themselves completely differently, making it confusing for shoppers and thereby reducing overall sales potential. One shop may have some kind of introduction page, another may open with special offers, whereas another may ask you what department you want. There is no consistency among online retailers, while offline stores provide a similar shopping experience. The confusion is confounded by the lack of testing and analysis for many online stores, meaning that a

website makes sense to the people who built it and run the business, but has little real impact on the hapless shopper, other than
to frustrate them or make them want to look for an alternative
supplier. The site has been designed from the inside out, rather
than the outside in.

The internet has spawned a couple of new industries over
the past decade or so, "usability" and "user experience design," or
UX as it is sometimes called. These functions include a great deal
of website testing to ensure that visitors can use your site easily
and that you can gain the maximum impact. Usability researchers
often conduct eye-tracking studies, as we have already discussed,
and "split testing," which allows designers to compare various
designs to see which work better in terms of, for example, "click-
through" rates, getting more people to click on the things you
want them to click on. Nevertheless, much of usability really is
common sense.

A blog post by usability expert Philip Webb, from the customer experience company Webcredible, offers an example.[21] Webb
compared the checkout process at UK-based retailer Next with that
at Amazon. He pointed out that when you arrive at the Next checkout and you are not logged in, you are presented with a form to
fill in.

If you have an account, filling in your name and password
lets you in and you can complete your purchase. However, as Webb
pointed out, people do not necessarily read any surrounding text:
they simply want to get on with their purchase as fast as possible.
So even if they do not have an account, they start filling in the
form, only to be frustrated when they get a page saying "Sorry, we
have been unable to sign you in." They won't have seen as easily an
invitation that appears on the right-hand side of the page inviting
visitors to register their details if they are new to Next. As Webb
said, "new customers are likely to believe that the sign-in fields are
the start of the registration process, and if they have an account or
not they would expect to move the process forward without enter-
ing new information on a new form."

In contrast, Amazon presents customers with a very clear
pathway for signing in, either as a "new" or "returning" customer.

You don't need any fancy testing to realize that people want to get through the checkout process quickly, and that obstacles to achieving this simply make buying less likely.

> TIP: Try to navigate your own online shop as though you know nothing about your company. Approach it with the eyes of a stranger looking to buy something. By doing this you can easily spot the obvious errors and problems.

Usability testing of some kind is essential for online shops, as it throws up some of the unexpected behaviors of potential shoppers. Furthermore, studies show that the perceived wisdom for how to design an online shop is not necessarily valid. For example, in a study comparing the reading of news in print and online, the Poynter Institute in Florida found that people read more text online than they do in print.[22] Yet the mantra from many web designers is that people read less text online. This simply is not the case, and indeed when people are in information-seeking mode, they expect to read. In addition, it is often claimed that people "scan" the page and do not read much of the text in between. However, the Poynter Institute study considered this specifically and found that people who scan web pages end up reading just the same amount of text as more methodical readers who go from top to bottom. If you leave your website design to chance or perceived wisdom, you could end up making poor choices and that, in turn, could lead to lower sales.

The Poynter Institute study also reveals another interesting aspect of how your online customers might surprise you. It is well known in the newspaper industry that large headlines and pictures are the elements that grab attention and get people moving around the pages. So if you were a newspaper company with years of experience in communicating in print, you might well expect that online you also need pictures and big headlines. Yet the Poynter Institute research shows that news consumers behave differently online – they employ other methods to guide them around the pages. Instead of headlines and pictures, they use navigation bars, menus, and drop-down items to find their way.

Shoppers don't all behave the same way

Shoppers vary considerably in the offline world, but their differences are much less easy to manage online. For instance, even though as we have seen many online shoppers are in information-seeking mode, others are not. What might be called the "utilitarian" customer wants to buy a specific product, and they want to buy it *now*. This presents a user experience problem for online retailers. If you build your website around information-seeking behaviors, the utilitarian visitor will not be satisfied. Equally, if you build your website the other way round, focusing on utilitarian visitors, then the information seeker will not be happy.

In real-world stores these two kinds of customers can more easily be accommodated. Sales staff can observe non-verbal behaviors and work out whether the person is trying to find a specific product or simply browsing, perhaps in need of some information or guidance. Online, there is no time for such intervention and a store has only a few seconds to show website visitors that it matches their behavior style. For instance, if you are the kind of shopper who likes to make comparisons between several alternatives, you want to see that the site enables this easily; if you are the kind of shopper who doesn't want to spend their time on comparisons, you don't want such options to get in your way of finding what you want to buy. If your online store's offering is not apparent to visitors, they are a mouse click away from an alternative that does meet their needs. It is not easy to produce one website that matches both behavior types.

In my consultancy work with businesses, this issue comes up repeatedly. If shoppers are going to make rapid decisions due to their short attention spans, how can a website be designed that matches all the individual requirements of all the specific kinds of shoppers?

You cannot do this; the only real option is to have multiple websites. Take UK business WorldStores, which won the 2012 "Multiple Site of the Year Award" from the Online Retail Association. It specializes in home furnishings and has several specialist or "niche" sites such as divanbedsworld.co.uk, woodenbedsworld.co.uk, and

barstoolworld.co.uk. Each has a clear and specific focus, meaning that if you are seeking "bar stools" or "divan beds" you know
immediately that you are on the right site. Even for someone with a
very short attention span, what the site does is obviously connected
to the visitor's specific requirements.

The company's owner, Joe Murray, revealed the importance
of this strategy in an interview with Rory Cellan-Jones, BBC
Technology Correspondent. He said:

> We looked though thousands of different keyword searches and
> spent two years analyzing the data to find categories that have
> a large volume of searches that don't really deliver a satisfactory
> result.[23]

People look for niches online, especially when they are utilitarian
shoppers, wanting to find a specific product or category and buy
straight away. Even so, the information-seeking behavior seen in
other online shoppers doesn't mean that having a niche site for
them isn't useful.

Barstoolworld.co.uk is clearly aimed at the utilitarian searcher who wants to buy a bar stool and buy it now. It appeals to people looking to buy and, through its name, also sets itself apart from the company's other furniture sites, such as divanbedsworld.co.uk. In other words, you can set up separate niche retail sites in one of two directions: either a product category niche, such as divan beds or bar stools; or a customer behavior niche, such as information seeking or buying now.

In an ideal world, retailers would produce niche websites that attracted buyers according to their behavior type as well as their product-specific requirements. However, this can be a significant management task and require additional staff to deal with a plethora of sites. In my discussions with businesses, the multiple-site approach is the one that business owners find most challenging, because it often demands different internal structures and new ways of working.

The problem is that while business owners such as this dither, their potential customers already live in a world of multiple sites. If your business cannot provide the kind of web experience people want, they can simply go elsewhere in the blink of an eye.

Online shopping is a multistore activity

Cast your mind back to the days before the internet, when you were shopping in your local town center. You might have had a list of items that reflected the order of the stores as you walked around. Sometimes you would go "off list" and visit other shops, perhaps because the item you wanted was out of stock, forcing you to find an alternative supplier, but you're not likely to have bothered to wander from shop to shop to compare prices. If the item was in stock and the price seemed reasonable, you would probably have bought the item from the first shop you visited. You would have traded saving money for convenience.

There is a strong psychological urge to do things with the least amount of effort. It is a primary survival instinct, helping us preserve energy for when it is needed, such as escaping a predator. That was important when we were evolving, of course, but is less of an issue these days. Even so, that instinct still hangs around in our brains, hence we rarely do more shopping than necessary. This means that real-world retailers can get away with things that their online counterparts cannot.

For instance, you can be $10 more expensive than your competition if they are a mile down the road, because people would rather pay you the additional money than go for a 20-minute walk. In contrast, if the competitor is next door, even a $1 price differential could make customers walk out and save the cash. In a study of food retailers in Sweden, researchers confirmed that prices were only sensitive when shops were close together.[24] Once shops were 1km apart or more, there was no real price competition.

Online, however, you don't have to go far or take much time to see whether you can get a better deal. Cheaper prices are only seconds away. With a click of the mouse or the swipe of a finger, you can leave one web shop and be in another. And unlike the real world of bricks and mortar, you don't have to go outside in the rain. The result of this ease and convenience is that people visit many more internet shops than they do bricks-and-mortar stores. Even in 2008 in the US, one in three online shoppers admitted to conducting more research and comparison than they had in the past.[25] With the preponderance of tablets, the increased capabilities of smartphones, and the general rise in online shopping, internet retailers can be certain that people are checking out alternative suppliers as a matter of course.

Shoppers' multistore activity is also having an impact on bricks-and-mortar outlets. One of my clients is a major motor dealer in the UK. Just five years ago the average number of car dealerships customers visited was eight; nowadays it is just over one. People used to visit several dealers to evaluate the cars on offer and towns often have hubs of dealers on their outskirts so people can easily walk from one dealership to the next. However, these days you can visit dealerships and car manufacturers online to work out the exact car you want, and then go to the dealer and buy it. This means that car dealers have eight times fewer face-to-face opportunities to sell than they used to have.

According to analysts like Experian and Ipsos, year-on-year retail footfall has fallen for many countries recently. The UK saw a reduction in people going to bricks-and-mortar stores of 4.5% between 2012 and 2013; in Hong Kong the fall was 2.9%, and in France it was 5.8%.[26] Some countries have had an increase in footfall, such as Portugal, but this followed a period of dramatic decrease in shopping due to the economic downturn after the banking crisis of 2008.

The online activity of bricks-and-mortar stores can thus be fundamental, because it can drive increased footfall into their real-world stores. For instance, an online store can build an email list of shoppers who are then sent an exclusive invitation to some kind of event in the local bricks-and-mortar store, or online shoppers can be given discount vouchers that can only be exchanged in physical shops. A greater web presence, more links online, and enhanced web visibility can help replace sales that could otherwise be lost.

Shoppers like easy comparisons

One way online retailers can prevent customers from wandering off to the competition is to make the comparisons for them, particularly for information-seeking customers.

However, for utilitarian shoppers who want a quick "have I made the right decision?" analysis, something along the lines of the ResponseNow[27] site fits the bill. This allows people to compare features and prices and prevents them from going away to a competitor's site. Columns could include the features of the items available. Comparisons could also detail prices as well as delivery terms and any added extras or bonuses on offer together with the original purchase. Remember, at the comparison stage of shopping people are not comparing benefits – they already know why they want to buy something. At this stage of decision-making shoppers are only interested in comparing features.

Fitting in with the internet shopper

So internet shopping has changed retail behavior, yet many retailers appear not to have realized this fundamental shift. Today's online shopper is information hungry, is seeking immediate gratification with a narrow span of attention, is often on the go, is looking at a small screen, and wants the best possible prices.

In fact this represents a significant opportunity for online retailers who can provide a mobile-friendly site that compares prices automatically, is usable, and is easy to work with. But there is one other factor that some online retailers have grasped as an important trend in online shopper behavior – loyalty.

In the past, for real-world stores, loyalty was usually born out of convenience. Alternative stores were in the wrong part of town or had expensive car parking or were too far away to walk. What these retailers claimed to be "loyalty" was often nothing of the kind; it was in fact a lack of desire on the part of shoppers to put themselves out. However, online it is so much easier to move away from a shop, even if you have previously been loyal to the firm or brand. Hence, one of the biggest ways of ensuring that your online store does well is to encourage true loyalty on the part of shoppers.

CASE STUDY: AMAZON

Amazon is an online store that benefits from an amazing degree of loyalty. Jeff Bezos, its founder, was a computer expert in Wall Street, New York, not someone with any retailing experience, yet his company has seen off competition from established, traditional retailers. According to one study of the number of visitors that go to online retailers, in America alone Amazon gets almost 2.5 times as many visitors as its nearest traditional retail rival, Walmart.[28]

So how has Amazon outshone companies with more retailing experience? Partly it is owing to "first-mover advantage." On the internet, the first company in a sector tends to do well. This is not always the case: search engines like Excite were around before Google came along, although Google was the first to rely on mathematics, rather than a human-compiled index, to help locate web pages. But while there had been some experiments with online malls where a collection of small stores were gathered together, Amazon was the first major individual store to set up online and capitalize on the opportunities of the web. Nevertheless, this is not the only factor: niche focus is important too. Sites that are focused on a niche can gain loyalty even if they are not the first to sell the kinds of items they stock.

Furthermore, loyalty is closely linked to the practical side of a website's functioning, its ease of use. Research in the US found that loyalty was heightened when people could readily navigate sites and find information quickly.[29] The study also established that stock availability and delivery flexibility were key features in gaining customer loyalty. In other words, online retailers who focus on usability and excellent logistics are the ones that customers prefer.

One final issue in terms of loyalty is offline branding. Amazon is all around – on posters, in newspaper adverts, in magazine articles. The name occurs as much in the real world as it does online. Similarly, eBay has a real-world identity, it is not merely an online shop. The top online retailers have spent a great deal of time and effort on public relations to brand their sites offline rather than using conventional marketing methods. Indeed, Google famously did not advertise on television until 2009, some 12 years after the company was formed.

If a particular retailer is on the tip of a shopper's tongue, it will be one of the first places they visit online. According to a story in the New York Times, "in 2009, nearly a quarter of shoppers started research for an online purchase on a search engine like Google and 18 percent started on Amazon."[30]

BLUEPRINT

Even though online retail is dominated by big brands such as eBay, it is possible to have a successful online store, particularly if your shop is in a narrow niche where you can dominate. If you understand and exploit how people shop online, your online store can be truly successful.

1. If your customers are information seekers, make sure your online store is packed with detailed information about your products. If your customers are utilitarian, make sure your site works perfectly so they can get what they want in a couple of clicks.
2. Ensure that your shop has extensive, capable, and visually obvious search facilities.
3. Make sure that your online shop is mobile friendly with a responsive design.
4. Use QR codes to increase customer interaction and provide more information.
5. Get your website analyzed using eye tracking and ensure that the "cold spots" have high emotional content that people will see in their peripheral vision.
6. Provide comparisons with other retailers to prevent people leaving your site for that information.
7. Develop a strong offline brand for your online shop.

4
IT'S ALL ABOUT PRICES

When Apple launched its revolutionary iPad at a price of $499, people were quick to speculate about how much it actually cost to make. They were curious about the level of profit the company was achieving. Manufacturing analysts were able to calculate that the total cost to Apple was around $260. Furthermore, the iPad that incorporated 3G mobile capability would have set you back a further $100, while the analysts claimed that the extra cost to Apple was a mere $16. Even though the price that consumers were charged for either iPad was substantially higher than the actual costs, Apple makes massive profits, and it does not offer discounts, people were still prepared to queue for hours to get the product. Price does not matter to these customers, it seems.

Meanwhile, Dollar Tree in the US and Poundland in the UK sell everything at a very low price – a single dollar or pound. Whatever you want to buy in these real-world stores, from soap to children's toys, the price is the same, just $1 or £1. Such shops are constantly busy as people seek the best possible price for everyday items. However, they can't raise their prices by even a single penny, because their customers do not expect to pay any more.

So why is it that people appear to be sensitive to prices when they are low, yet happy to pay over the odds for other items, even when they know the company they are buying from could afford to lower the price? You'd think consumers would always seek out the lowest price and avoid paying too much for an item, but that is not the case. What is more, some of the items you can buy in Poundland are actually cheaper in nearby supermarkets, perhaps 97p; this is one way discount stores make a profit. When it comes to pricing, buyers' behavior is not rational or logical.

> The price charged for an item is a relatively minor influence in the decision to buy.

Psychological priming of price expectation

If price is not the deciding factor, what else is influencing the con-sumer? The first is something known as psychological priming.

When you visit a bricks-and-mortar Apple Store, whether on New York's Fifth Avenue or London's Regent's Street, the first thing you notice is that it looks and feels expensive. Not only are the stores beautiful, spacious, and bright, they are also full of staff. The whole place has a feeling of purpose, service, and luxury. The Apple website also has the look and feel of extravagance, with multimedia design that many other websites try to imitate but do not quite manage to pull off. There is plenty of white space, for instance, and color is only used for emphasis, the rest of the site being white and gray. Furthermore, you can watch videos or listen to audio clips without having to leave the site – it is all presented seamlessly.

Meanwhile, the Dollar Tree and Poundland websites are sim-ple and functional. They include stickers to emphasize the low prices you are paying, and allow you to fill your online shopping cart quickly with all the low-priced items you want. These com-panies do not emphasize luxury at all, and hence you expect only low prices.

Despite their differences, both kinds of businesses are priming their shoppers. When you are in an expensive shop, you expect to pay higher prices. Apple can charge higher prices because it has raised our expectations and primed us to expect to pay more because of the expensive, luxury feel of its stores and its website. When you visit a store or a website that is much more spartan, you expect to pay lower prices.

This phenomenon can also be observed in restaurants. You can get a burger and chips at a low price in a typical franchise chain, or you can get almost exactly the same kind of food for five times the price in a nearby family restaurant. For instance, McDonald's prides itself on delivering food fast. It creates an environment with bright lights and colors, plastic trays, and so on emphasizing that the restaurant is not a place to linger over your food, or somewhere you might go for a special occasion. Meanwhile, on the same street will be a restaurant that has tablecloths, with waiter service and an atmosphere that suggests you're welcome to stay for ages and while away the hours, yet it may still offer a simple burger and chips. For similar food we pay far higher prices because we have been primed to pay those amounts, even though the ingredients of the meal are roughly equivalent.

> TIP: If you want people to pay high prices on your website, prime them into expecting to do so: make sure your website exudes luxury.

Priming is not only about the environment you create, it is about all the other signals you send about price. The kind of price sticker you use, the way you display your prices, the color of the text in which the price is displayed, even the position of the price tags on web pages all affect the perception people have of the prices you charge.

On the Apple online store, for instance, when a shopper wants to buy an iPad, the price is initially displayed in a subtle gray, only becoming emboldened in black once the specific model has been selected. Even then, it is only in the same type size as the main text of the page, with a "buying button" that is green and says simply "Continue." It does not shout "buy me now" or emphasize that you are parting with almost $1,000. However, over at BuyCheapSoftware.com, the prices are big and bold with busy pages, little white space, and huge "Buy" buttons.

Customers have an impact on prices

Part of the priming process involves letting your customers know who else buys your products and services. If a website visitor thinks they are in the company of millionaires before they see the prices, then they expect them to be high. If, however, your website indicates in some way that the people who visit it are those with less disposable income, perhaps with images of people in "ordinary" circumstances, consumers are primed into thinking that the prices will be low.

In an intriguing study, researchers at the University of Texas primed people to consider the kind of company they would be keeping if they were to buy a broadband installation from an internet service provider.[1] The prices other people had paid were shown to the potential purchasers. Previous customers were said to have paid $440, whereas those involved in the research could get the identical service for a mere $280, saving themselves $160. Interestingly, most people didn't want to get the cost savings. This was partly because the participants in the research felt the company was being unfair to its existing customers, but another influencing factor was again to do with priming – if you are told that you are in the company of people who pay high prices, you expect and want to pay high prices. Otherwise, you are not the same as "them."

So one good thing online retailers can do is to demonstrate that their website has the kind of people using it that a visitor expects. Social media add-ons such as a Facebook panel showing who "likes" the shop can help, as can images of those who use the site in the environment that confirms what sort of people they might be – high-price sites might have images of their customers on yachts or beside expensive cars. Watch retailer WF&C, for instance, has images of its classy London store on its website and photos of craftspeople taking care of watches on its Facebook page, combining to make people expect high prices. Meanwhile, the Watchshop website is focused less on making you feel you are in the company of high-rollers and more that you are associating yourself with those who are seeking value.

> TIP: Use social media technology to reveal the kind of customers who buy from your website. This will help set price expectations through priming.

One further overarching priming factor needs to be considered: consumers believe that the internet itself is a lower-cost environment. A study conducted by Taiwanese researchers showed that in general people expect prices on the internet to be 8% lower than in physical stores.[2] Partly this is because people think that overheads are lower online and therefore companies can pass on the cost savings. It is also due to the fact that people have become acclimatized to lower prices on the web. This means that companies conducting business online are somewhat hampered by the priming effect of the internet itself.

Choosing the right numbers for prices

Whether on- or offline, business owners naturally want to make sure they can sell as much as possible at the highest price people will pay. But how high is the highest? There is plenty of myth and assumption surrounding the notion that businesses will get more buyers if they price something at £9.99 than if they were to sell it at £10. They may lose a penny on each sale, but they make up for that small drop in price by selling more items.

Nevertheless, is there any real evidence that pricing like this actually works? And should businesses be using different final numbers instead of 9 anyway? After all, many business owners are convinced that ending the price in 5 or even 7 is also likely to produce more sales.

Odd-numbered pricing has been used for decades, but in recent years a new "golden" pricing number has emerged – 7. It still follows the odd-number "rule," but instead of seeing things on sale on the internet for prices such as $199 or $195, you mostly see them for $197. There is much speculation as to why this might be, but what seems to have happened is that one internet marketing "guru" tested the sales of products at different prices and discovered that a $197 sale price led to more profit. He shared his finding with other internet marketers, who copied his preference for prices ending in a 7. That led to swathes of the internet being plastered in price tags ending in 7, and other businesses assumed that this must be the best number online.

One test, by one person, in one market situation is not substantial evidence. And in fact, properly conducted scientific research tells another story. It suggests that the last digit of a price is much less important than the first digit. In a study at New York University, researchers found that when a price is rounded down customers think it is much cheaper than it actually is because of the impact the rounding has on the first digit.[3] Consider an item priced at £200. If you round that down to £199.99, customers logically know that this is just one penny short of the actual price, but the first digit is now half the value. This appears to make us think that the price is much lower than it actually is. Similarly, if you have an item at $4.99 instead of $5, it appears much cheaper because $4 is 20% cheaper than $5.

There is also some evidence that we tend to round down odd numbers and round up even ones. If something is priced at £19.97 we tend to round that down to a more "normal" number, such as £19.95, implying that the price is cheaper. But if the price were £19.98 we round it up, meaning we would perceive that as £19.99, so more expensive. Because odd numbers tend to be rounded down, people think they are getting a better deal.

> Odd numbers feel smaller than even ones because we view them as descending, whereas even numbers are seen as going upward.

Another aspect of digits is the sound they make in our heads when we read them. Try saying out loud "nine ninety nine," and then say "nine ninety seven". The chances are it takes you fractionally longer to say 9.99 than 9.97 because we tend to lengthen long vowel sounds, as in "ine," whereas the "ev" and "en" of 7, even though they comprise two syllables, are quite short vowel sounds. If the price sounds short, we think the price is low. If the price sounds long, we think it is high. This could explain why $197 is more effective than $195, because the higher price actually sounds smaller.

Furthermore, research has shown that certain consonants in the words that make up the sounds of numbers are associated with a perception of relative value. For example, words containing the letters "s" and x" sound smaller than those containing "v" and "n."

This all suggests that the word "six" should be perceived as relatively small, because it contains two small-sounding consonants and a short vowel sound. Hence, if you ended your prices with 6 you might gain additional sales. But 6, of course, is an even number, so it tends to be rounded up to 7 in a price such as $196.

Thus the way we think about the numbers in a particular price is complex and is based on the following features:

◆ The value of the first digit.
◆ Whether the last digit is odd or even.
◆ Rounding up even numbers and rounding down odd numbers.
◆ The length of the vowel sounds in the digits.
◆ The consonants that make up the digits.

As a result, choosing the right price, both on- and offline, is a complex business and requires market testing.

How price displays affect buyers

How prices are physically displayed also has an influence on the likelihood of sales. For example, which is the better deal here?

SPECIAL OFFER	
Was £24.99	Now **£19.99**
Was **£24.99**	Now £19.99

Both price displays actually offer the same discount. However, we perceive the top one as less of a deal than the bottom example. In the top row, the display emphasizes the lower price in larger type, whereas the bottom example highlights the previous (higher) price. The type size used influences what we think of the numbers. In the top example, the bigger number is the lower price, so as a result we get confused and think we aren't getting such a great deal. In the second example, the size of the type is proportional to the deal we are receiving (that is, it decreases in size according to value) and research confirms that when the type size of prices is appropriate people buy more. In other words, if you are discounting prices the reduced price should be in smaller type than the original, larger price. Many stores make the mistake of emphasizing the new lower price in bigger type, but people perceive this as a higher price because it is physically larger.

> TIP: Show prices in type sizes that are proportional to each other – big prices in large type sizes and lower prices in smaller type sizes.

The color of the type in which prices are displayed can also have an influence on whether or not people perceive the item to be good value. Amazon, for instance, displays its prices in red. At first sight this may seem counter-intuitive, because in many cultures red is a signal to stop, so you might think it puts people off buying. But in fact, the color red is partly why Amazon succeeds. Red is a color that in nature signals the need to act fast – it is a color for sexual display in some animals, for example – so people are more likely to press the "add to basket" button if the price displayed is in red rather than, say, green, which might more logically be associated with action, like the "Go" of a traffic light.

Nevertheless, research conducted at the Saïd Business School at the University of Oxford suggests that red may not always be the best color for prices. This study showed that the impact of prices in red was far greater on men than it was on women. Indeed, the color of the price was relatively unimportant in terms of women's buying behavior. So if most of your customers are women, then displaying your prices in red may have a neutral impact on sales.

The impact on men, in contrast, could tie into basic psychology, with men being primed to focus on this color as a means of finding a mate. Red is a potent sexual signal – think of attracting men with red lipstick, or even of the rear end of a female baboon, which becomes more red when the animal is ready to mate. So if you have male customers, putting your prices in red may encourage them to buy quickly.

The actual position of pricing information is also crucial to making people want to buy. When we are focused on the left of something we tend to think it is smaller than when we are leaning toward the right.[4] This implies that if a business puts prices on the right-hand side of a web page it is leading people to think that the price is higher than it actually is. This is also important in bricks-and-mortar stores: price tags ought to be on the left side of products, making people feeling that the price is smaller and hence encouraging sales.

Discounting and its impact on sales

Negotiation expert Derek Arden is always seeking a "discount." Indeed, he appeared on television in the UK showing how easy it was to negotiate deals up and down the High Street in Guildford, Surrey. Known as "Mr Negotiator," Derek can get a deal when the rest of us think it's impossible.

I remember being at a dinner with Derek and four business leaders at a posh London hotel. Derek was hosting the dinner and had arranged for wine to be on the table in advance. When we sat down we looked at the menu while the waiter poured some wine. Derek chatted to the waiter, noticed his name badge, and called him by name. He then leaned toward the waiter, smiled at him, and thanked him for being so attentive to his guests. Later, after the waiter had taken the food orders, Derek called him across and quietly said we would need more wine. But then, using the waiter's first name, he pointed out that he didn't really have the budget for an extra two bottles, only one, but that would seem somewhat stingy to his guests. His boss was limiting his budget, he said, so was there anything the waiter could do to help him? After a few more moments of friendly conversation, the waiter replied, "Certainly, sir, I shall see what I can do." He came back with two bottles of wine, but Derek was only charged for one. Yet Derek didn't specifically ask for this, nor did he request a discount. He merely chatted in a friendly way and asked the waiter what could be done to help him out of his budgetary problem.

One of the key factors in Derek's wine deal was the rapport he established with the waiter. Once you make a friend of some-one who is trying to sell you something, it is difficult for them not to have some kind of emotional attachment to you. In turn, that means that if you blame an external person for your situation when you can't afford the price, the salesperson wants to try to help you because they feel for you. These are key tactics in negotiations: building rapport and placing the power external to the situation.

Online, however, this sort of interaction is impossible. How do customers build rapport with online stores to try to get a better deal? And how can retailers offer discounts online without creating an expectation of them, or without making the store look cheap and tacky because it always has discounts?

Business strategist Janet Switzer discusses this point in her book *Instant Income*:

> I personally do not like discounting the price of anything, as I think it sends the wrong message to your prospects. After all, if you don't think your product or service is worth anything, guess what? A lot of other people won't think so, either.[5]

Leading American sales expert Jeffrey Gitomer backs this up with his assertion that "74% of price cuts are started by salespeople – not customers."[6] In other words, discounting is often the result of businesses thinking that their prices are too high for their customers, or making the assumption that people will not pay without a discount. Discounting and lower prices are often born out of irrational fear on the part of retailers rather than customer demand.

And almost everywhere you look in online retail, there are discounts. Indeed, the mighty eBay proudly displays discounted prices so you can see you're getting a bargain. It even has a "You Save" notice displaying the actual amount and the percentage saved to emphasize the fact.

In Australia, online store OO does something similar, but emphasizes the discount even more by stating the percentage saving and adding a "combine and save" option.

So if it is good for eBay and OO, should your online store follow suit, in spite of the reservations that sales experts have about the general principle of discounting?

Research conducted at Penn State University in Philadelphia provides an interesting twist to this debate. The study found little evidence that people are sensitive to prices online.[7] However, what it did reveal was that the internet encourages more price searching – so people do search for lower prices, but price is actually only one factor in their decision to buy. Thus discounts may not be as important as online retailers think they are.

Coupons are equally popular online. The biggest supplier of coupons to the UK supermarket sector is a company called Valassis. It looked at coupon usage between 2010 and 2012 and showed significant growth year on year, an increase of 40% from 2011 to 2012.[8] Furthermore, a 2012 study from Valassis determined that 74% of people searched multiple online coupon providers each week.

Nevertheless, a study from Memphis State University that looked at the motivation for gaining discounts discovered that getting a lower price was only of minor significance. The main motivation was to beat the supplier. The researchers said, "the pride and satisfaction of obtaining savings through the use of coupons was found to be the most important determinant of coupon usage."[9] They went on to point out that perhaps it would be more appropriate for stores to emphasize the sense of accomplishment people would feel if they used a discount coupon, instead of stressing the price saving.

There are well over 1,000 websites offering discount coupons, such as RetailMeNot, Coupons.com, and MyVoucherCodes. Between them, they attract hundreds of millions of visitors every day. In an interview with *Business Insider*, the owners of RetailMeNot revealed that in 2011, just two years after launch, the company had $80m in revenues.[10] Most of that income is derived from advertising, but around 10% comes from commissions paid by the companies providing the coupons. Clearly, both shoppers and retailers are interested in discount codes.

Retailers seem to believe that discounting brings in more business and more website traffic. However, research from Vanderbilt University in Nashville shows that websites that use discount codes may well be reducing their profitability.[11] Far from triggering a desire to buy, the presence of coupons appears to diminish the chances of people buying.

> TIP: To increase your profitability online, avoid blatant discounts. They have the reverse effect to what many retailers think.

My friend Derek didn't get a discount, because five-star hotels don't offer them. He did, however, get a deal, which allowed him to feel he had achieved something, while ensuring the hotel could continue its policy of no discounts and thereby retain its luxury status. Deals and discounts are very different things, and deals in fact appear to be better for both sides of the selling and buying relationship. You need to be creative: rather than offering money-off discounts, suggest that people can get more for their money, such as a deal that incorporates shipping charges if they spend over a certain amount, or one where they can get additional items to accompany what they have in their shopping basket.

Are special offers worth it?

Special offers should not be confused with discounts. Even though a special offer may involve a reduced price, most special offers are associated with another feature, such as limited availability or a narrow time window. They frequently appeal to the psychological notion of scarcity: people put a higher value on things that are scarce than on things that are abundant.

Psychologist Robert Cialdini from Arizona State University has devoted his academic life to the study of persuasion, and has identified that scarcity is an important aspect in persuading shoppers to buy an item. In his book *Persuasion: The Psychology of Influence*, he tells the story of a couple in an electrical appliance store who are obviously keen on a particular product.[12] After watching the couple for a while, the salesperson goes over and says that only 20 minutes earlier he had sold the last one in the store to another couple. The people looking at the appliance were clearly disappointed, but that made it even more likely they would buy the only remaining item, the one on display.

We have all been there: we are interested in buying something and are dithering about purchase until we see the sign saying "last few remaining," "only three left," or something similar. Once we see that, we are much more likely to buy due to the apparent scarcity of the item. Evolutionary psychologists explain this as being a basic survival instinct. Hundreds of thousands of years ago, when the human race was developing, food was the focus of our day. We needed to gather in or hunt for the items that kept us alive. If food was scarce, it became more important to us in our chances of survival, and so its relative value rose. Our brains became used to associating scarcity with high value – something that persists today, even though food is not in short supply for most people in the Western world.

There are several ways you can emphasize scarcity online. Some stores show the stock availability for particular products. The popular ecommerce program Magento includes a number of extensions that allow this to be done in various creative ways. One such extension, from the company aheadWorks, allows a bar to be shown that clearly demonstrates falling stock levels, making it much more likely that people will want to buy.

In situations like this, the price becomes much less significant to the buyer: the scarcity of the item makes it seem more valuable than the cost would suggest. As a result, the price seems lower because the shopper values the item more highly: this is a truly "special offer" to them.

Scarcity can also be suggested with prices or products that are only available for a limited amount of time. Bricks-and-mortar retailers do this with events like a "Blue Cross Sale," popularized by British department store Debenhams. Items are marked with a blue cross for one day only, and on that day they have more deeply discounted prices. Such sales get people into the store, but it is the apparent lack of availability that triggers the interest of buyers, not the low prices.

TIP: If you emphasize scarcity you can get more sales, even at higher prices, thereby increasing profits.

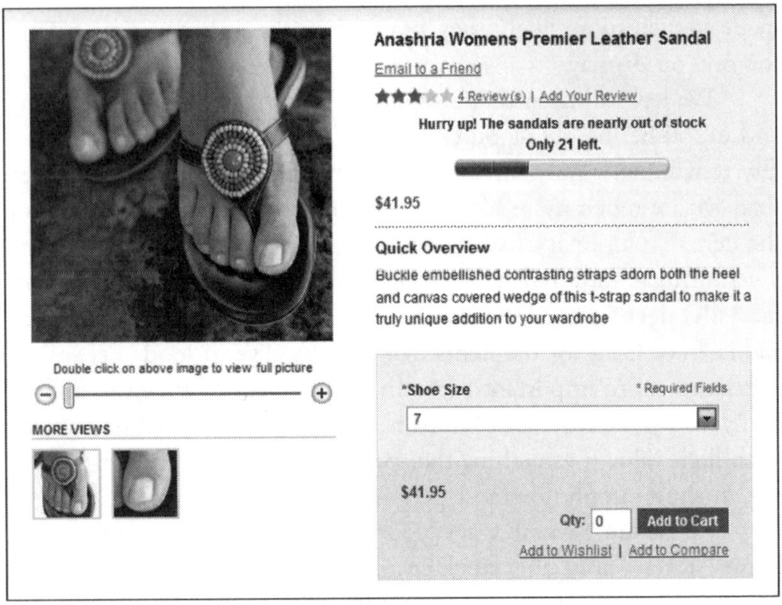

Anashria Womens Premier Leather Sandal

Email to a Friend

★★★☆☆ 4 Review(s) | Add Your Review

Hurry up! The sandals are nearly out of stock
Only 21 left.

$41.95

Quick Overview

Buckle embellished contrasting straps adorn both the heel and canvas covered wedge of this t-strap sandal to make it a truly unique addition to your wardrobe

Double click on above image to view full picture

⊖ ⊕

MORE VIEWS

*Shoe Size   * Required Fields

7

$41.95

Qty: 0   Add to Cart

Add to Wishlist | Add to Compare

Image courtesy of www.aheadworks.com

CASE STUDY: GROUPON

On the Internet the whole concept of limited-time offers has been turned into a multimillion-pound business by Groupon. This began in 2008 as a "deal of the day" website for people based in Chicago. It provided special offers for local people, which they could buy in stores in their area. The Groupon system expanded to Boston, New York, and Toronto before going global in 2010. Although Groupon itself disappointed its early investors, it has over half the share of the daily deals market online, with its nearest competitor, LivingSocial, only achieving around half the monthly revenue. Groupon works on the scarcity principle. Deals may well be lower in price, but the desire to buy is influenced by the bold "countdown" sign that lets visitors know how little time they have left to buy the deal.

This kind of special offer is immensely appealing. Even individuals setting up their own blog can sell things employing the scarcity principle, using software such as Scarcity Samurai, from the Australian company Noble Samurai. This allows anyone with the WordPress content management system to inject a variety of scarcity techniques into their web pages. These include a one-time only offer, as well as a countdown timer to when the offer ends. Special offers like this are a highly valuable way of increasing online sales and have a much greater psychological hook than a mere price discount.

This all makes great sense for individual stores providing their own deals on their own sites, but the multitude of special offers on daily deal sites can have an impact on online retailers as a whole, as it means people may well wait until they find a deal. Thus daily deal sites may actually be suppressing sales as people hang back from buying. David Rose, who runs a New York investment fund, told the website *Young Entrepreneur* that daily deals might well work for the consumer, but not necessarily for the shop itself:

I'm not sure it legitimately works out for the vendor because people who are trapping for a discount are typically not the kind of life cycle customer that you want to get. They're typically one-shot, in and out.[13]

Harvard Business School also expressed some skepticism about daily deal websites. It said that in spite of the fact there are some benefits in offering limited-time special deals, it isn't possible to stop customers getting multiple vouchers. Profits could be hit as customers simply wait for deals and use their vouchers on the appropriate dates. If you do want to use daily deals, whether through Groupon, another daily deal site, or on your own website, it seems better to emphasize scarcity rather than low prices. That way you can retain profitability; indeed, you could possibly increase it as people would value your items more because they appear to be rare and then simple supply-and-demand economics come into play.

Special offers provided by email rather than on websites can be particularly valuable. In a 2011 study by analysts Nielsen, special offers were the main reason people wanted to follow a brand on a social network.[14] This is backed by research reported in *Marketing Magazine* in 2012, which showed that special offers were the main reason people opened marketing emails from companies.[15] However, a study in India found that there appears to be a generational difference when it comes to special offers. Researchers from the Amity Business School, Uttar Pradesh, discovered that special-offer emails were opened mostly by those aged over 30.[16] This suggests that if your website does provide special offers, or you send them via email to your mailing list, you are likely to get better results from older customers than younger ones. There is also evidence from a study in America that men are less likely than women to be interested in special offers such as coupons.[17] So simplistically, you are going to make the most of special offers if you target women over 30.

According to the shopper behavior expert Phillip Adcock, the special offer itself is subject to a considerable array of different psychological factors, including unconscious mental processing, conscious thinking about what to buy, and the use of different parts of our brain simultaneously when we go shopping.[18] Consequently, little beats specific testing in individual markets under particular circumstances. If you want to make the most of special offers in your online store, you are going to have to test them. Indeed, testing all the elements of pricing displays is essential to ensure you obtain the best results.

The easiest way to test every aspect of your pricing is to use A/B split testing. To do this you set up two pages to compare the element you are considering, such as a special offer. One page contains the special offer price, the other does not. You then deliver the first page to the first web visitor and the alternative page to the second visitor. You give the first page to the third visitor and the second page to the fourth visitor and so on, alternating the two pages from one visitor to the next. Google provides software to do this through its Analytics service. After running the test for a while, you will be able to see what impact there has been on sales.

The consequences of dynamic pricing

Dynamic pricing is immensely popular with online retailers. This is when the prices displayed to individual customers are amended according to a range of different factors and analyzed in real time by database software, which then produces a particular price for a particular customer. The factors that are used in this analysis can be the frequency with which the customer has visited the site, how popular an individual item is on a specific day, and the current prices on competing websites. Prices can also be changed according to demand. This happens frequently in the travel industry, with ticket prices increasing as supply goes down. Each time someone buys a ticket online, the price displayed on the relevant web page goes up automatically.

Dynamic pricing clearly has significant benefits for retailers. It is convenient, automatic, and can help make certain items more profitable. However, consumers are gradually becoming aware that dynamic pricing is in place and can react negatively to it.

Amazon started testing dynamic pricing with DVDs in 2000. It received a considerable negative reaction, with people claiming it was unfair to charge some people as much as $15 more than another customer buying an identical item. Even so, five years later, CNN reported that most people still had no idea that the prices they were offered online could vary considerably. Seven years after that, in 2012, the *Wall Street Journal* investigated dynamic pricing and found it to be widespread, even though 76% of consumers objected to it.[19] There are even popular websites explaining how to avoid dynamic pricing and its sometimes higher prices.

So while your website may well be able to offer dynamic pricing and increase its profitability as a result, there is the possibility of negative consequences and doing so could influence how fair your business is perceived to be by potential customers.

The likelihood that dynamic pricing could affect the perception of an online store was considered by researchers at the University of Maryland. In their study of the importance of dynamic pricing for customer behavior, they said:

> Consumers expect posted prices to remain constant over a reasonable time and across consumers, and will cease to trust the vendor if they find that they have been discriminated against through dynamic pricing.[20]

They suggest that transparency is key. Indeed, one way of dealing with dynamic pricing is to provide different prices to specific kinds of customers, but to be obvious about what you are doing. For example, sites offer different prices to customers with loyalty cards or membership than they do to non-members or those without loyalty cards. Similarly, Microsoft and Adobe both have academic pricing strategies in place offering their downloadable software at substantially lower prices for students and academics than for the general buyer. This kind of dynamic pricing is transparent and obvious, and is therefore more acceptable than the "secret" or hidden dynamic pricing that many online stores want to follow.

An alternative transparent method of dynamic pricing is also used in the utilities sector. Here, pricing can vary according to the estimated amount of power that the customer will use in the next year, for example how much home insulation they have and the extent of the energy-saving activities they are prepared to undertake. By answering several questions, consumers can see how the price they are charged changes. A similar transparent method of dynamic pricing is also used in the telecommunications sector, where telephone line prices can alter depending on such factors as whether or not you are prepared to pay any money up front.

> TIP: If you want to set dynamic prices on your website to respond to market conditions, you will gain trust if you are transparent about what you are doing.

The problems with price comparison

As we have seen, the internet has enabled people to discover easily whether prices are different from one geographical location to another, or one website to another. It doesn't take more than a few mouse clicks to check the prices of different suppliers, or discover unfair pricing strategies. This was the case in 2011 when Adobe launched its Creative Suite 5.5 software as an online service. Instead of buying a physical disk, you could simply rent the software online. However, as the magazine *PC Pro* revealed, you could rent the software in the US for $129 (then equivalent to £78), yet in the UK the price was £139.20, including 20% VAT. In the past, software companies have been able to claim that pricing in the UK needs to be higher because their programs require localizing linguistically, because there are additional shipping costs they need to cover, and because they face deeper discounting from retailers. However, as *PC Pro* pointed out, the software was an online service provided directly from the developer: it therefore did not have some of these additional costs that contribute to a higher price.

A similar debate about Adobe's pricing strategy began in Australia, where the pricing of the software was also substantially higher compared to America. However, it led the government there to launch an inquiry into IT pricing. Just before that began,

Adobe lowered its Australian prices to match the American fees. So even if companies believe they have the right to charge different prices in different countries, the internet prevents this from occurring as soon as people realize what is happening or believe it is unfair. It has made people much more price conscious, although they are not necessarily looking for the cheapest prices, just price fairness.

The ability to compare prices quickly from one website to another has led to the development of price comparison sites that allow people to visit one aggregated site to obtain price comparisons, instead of having to surf the web themselves to check out a variety of different stores. The first price comparison site, PriceWatch, was launched as long ago as 1995, but the sector did not really take off until 2000 with sites such as Shopping.com, PriceGrabber, and Shopzilla, which are the biggest price comparison sites in the world. In Europe the leader is Kelkoo, and in Australia it is Getprice.

There are now also specialist sector sites, such as Trivago for hotels or comparethemarket.com for financial services. However, these sites earn their money from the companies they list, which pay either a flat fee to be included or a commission based on each click received via the price comparison site. In other words, online retailers are paying price comparison sites to make sure they get visitors who want cheaper prices. Yes, that's what happens: shops are paying other websites to find them customers who want to spend less money!

One way out of this for retailers using such systems is to create high "reference" prices. This means that the recommended retail price, for instance, is artificially inflated, and the "discounted" prices therefore seem excellent bargains. However, as researchers at Nottingham University Business School suggested when they investigated package holiday prices, people are skeptical of high reference prices on comparison sites, and this leads to "potential behavioural impacts."[21] What this really means is that if companies using price comparison sites set high recommended prices and then offer deep discounts, consumers are more wary and less likely to buy.

Furthermore, an analysis of a comparison website for the insurance sector suggested that the pressure to compete has led many insurance companies to offer products for prices that are uneconomic unless the customer buys additional products or carries on with the insurance for a second year.

Price comparisons are not necessarily good for consumers either. In Italy in 2007, the government passed a law that meant that car drivers should be provided with price comparison notifications for fuel. Petrol and diesel prices from competing filling stations are displayed on roadside signs, as well as on the internet. The prices are constantly updated, providing drivers with an instant signal as to where the cheapest fuel can be bought. The notion behind this law was that the competitive nature of the pricing displays would force the oil companies to keep their prices low, thereby benefiting the consumer. However, research found that this was not the case.[22] Instead, prices went up by 1 cent on average, compared with the government-predicted fall of 8 cents. The researchers are not sure why this was the case, but a likely explanation is contractual arrangements between oil companies and fuel retailers that actually prevent market-led price competition.

Furthermore, even though online it is possible to compare prices easily, it is something of a distraction. Once the comparison is made, people still doubt whether anything is a true bargain. Plus, they frequently buy from stores they would have bought from anyway, even if the price from their favorite or trusted store is a few pounds or dollars higher. They are merely checking that they are not being ripped off with excessive prices. In this case, all the price comparison site achieves is a lower profit for the online store because it brings in customers at a fee who were going to visit the store anyway.

An indication of the lack of effectiveness of price comparison sites is given in the recommendations for how consumers should use them, produced by the Advertising Standards Authority in the UK. These tell people to use more than one price comparison site, to make sure that the comparisons are fair, and to read the small print. If shoppers have to do so much work themselves, price comparison becomes considerably less convenient and therefore much less attractive as a proposition.

Do prices matter?

Several years ago, one of my clients was ICI Paints, then the manufacturer of the Dulux brand. At one meeting I attended I was somewhat taken aback by the company accountant's bold assertion that prices do not matter. At that time, Dulux was charging more than twice the price of its main competition, own-brand paints supplied by the large DIY and home improvement stores. Yet it had twice their market share. If price mattered, said the accountant, people would be flocking to the considerably cheaper paint products. What did matter, he said, was a combination of quality and brand perception. Dulux was a quality paint and the brand was well respected. As a result, people were willing to pay a premium price.

Many retailers think price matters when to consumers it is of secondary importance. In my local supermarket there are display tickets below products pointing out the price in competing stores. Often the prices are a penny or two cheaper in the shop I visit, but occasionally they are higher than in an alternative store. But why would I get in my car and drive a mile or two in an attempt to save a few pennies? The supermarket is focusing my mind on price when it does not need to, and there is only a marginal possibility that it might make me think I am getting great value.

> TIP: Focus your customers' minds on the values of your brand; that way you will avoid the need to consider lowering your prices.

BLUEPRINT

People make their mind up in seconds whether or not to purchase something, so the way pricing is displayed is a fundamental component of getting a sale. Display prices poorly and you will reduce your sales.

1. Prime people to expect the right kind of price. If you want them to feel they will be getting low prices, make sure your website does not look too well designed or expensive.
2. Use prices that end in an odd number.
3. Make the sound of your prices short if you wish to emphasize value.
4. Display prices proportionally, with lower prices in smaller type.
5. Consider the color of your prices – red can sometimes lead to more sales.
6. Avoid price discounts – they are not as valuable as many retailers think.
7. Ensure that you emphasize scarcity through showing stock levels and/or special offers.
8. Dynamic pricing, if in place, needs to be transparent to avoid loss of trust.
9. Avoid price comparisons; instead focus your shoppers' minds on the values of your brand.

5
SHOPPING CARTS GET ABANDONED

Imagine you are in a supermarket wandering around the aisles, filling up your shopping trolley as you go. You get to the checkout and just as you are about to unload your items onto the conveyor belt, you change your mind. You simply leave your trolley at the checkout and walk out of the store. What is more, you are not the only person to behave like this. What if over half the people in the shop did the same as you? Can you imagine the chaos if all around the world there were millions of abandoned shopping baskets and trolleys? Even worse, can you imagine the costs for the shops themselves? There would be the expense of the loss of perishable foods for a start, such as frozen food that defrosted, as well as the need for extra staff to put things back on shelves. On top of that, the shops would be cluttered with trolleys and baskets and so customers would be put off going in. The result would be fewer sales, making prices even higher. Bricks-and-mortar retailers do everything in their power to stop this from happening: they ensure that plenty of tills are open, that they have self-scanning cash desks to avoid queueing, and that there are staff available to help us find the fastest lane.

Yet internet retailers appear happy to let us abandon our shopping carts with glee. In fact, between 60% and 74% of all shopping carts online get abandoned.[1] Right at the point when people have almost finished their shopping, just at the moment they're about to get their credit card out of their pocket and pay, they say "Nah, can't be bothered" and off they go to visit somewhere else online, leaving their shopping cart lurking in the ether. Worse than this, the online retail sector appears to be oblivious to what is happening.

What are the reasons for shoppers abandoning their online carts so frequently?

The online shopping cart is cumbersome

One of the problems is that most online shopping carts are cumbersome and awkward.

What if you went into a real-world shop, picked up some items, then walked to the checkout, only to be told when you got there that you couldn't pay for the items until you'd given your name and password? You don't have to log in to bricks-and-mortar stores, yet thousands of online shops require you to do so, adding an additional step to the purchasing process.

Then you are asked for all sorts of details before you can pay, such as your home address, your phone number, and so on. You can pay with the same credit card in a physical store without having to provide any of these personal details. Indeed, four out of ten people abandon shopping carts because the system wants too much information or they need to log in first.

Of course some of this information is necessary for delivery and some is for our own protection, but one study found that the average shopping process online takes between five and six separate pages.[2] You can't call that convenient.

Auction site eBay has led the way in allowing people to purchase without registering first. You can buy as a "guest," without logging in beforehand or providing any details. True, there are some restrictions, such as the maximum price of the item or the number of times you can use the guest service. Even with these limitations, though, it is far less hassle.

Other shopping cart software providers have followed suit such as osCommerce, which allows online stores to sell things without requiring their visitors to register. Not all business owners know about such facilities, of course, and some ignore them because they want you to sign up to their newsletters and the like. But with such features becoming more widely available, we can expect to see a rising number of stores offering more convenient shopping carts.

One particular problem that does require attention is that few shopping carts work well on mobile devices, leading to further high levels of abandonment. In fact, mobile phone shopping carts are generally dreadful, even when compared with ordinary carts.

They require people to click, instead of being geared to touch, and they use drop-down menus, which are difficult to navigate with a finger. According to one study, a whopping 97% of shopping carts accessed by mobile phones are abandoned.[3] This is an area in which technology suppliers are investing a great deal of effort, and retailers need to follow suit.

Unexpected payment problems

When we shop, we like to know what to expect before we pay. In most real-world stores you can see the credit card signs on the windows, although you don't really need to look at them, because almost every shop accepts every form of payment. That is not the case online.

Some online retailers don't even accept credit cards, they force you to send a check or pay using a bank transfer – but they don't tell you that until you have collected your items and have your shopping cart ready at the checkout.

Even if the site announces proudly "Pay with your credit card," you can get to the checkout only to find that the brand of credit card you possess is not acceptable to the shop. Some online retailers only accept Visa, for example, which is an issue if you only have a MasterCard.

Research indicates that 7 out of every 100 shopping baskets online are abandoned because the shopper discovered at the checkout that there were not enough payment options for them.

Shipping makes people angry

Another problem is getting all the way to the checkout and then discovering that there are going to be additional charges for delivery or, worse still, that the shipping charges are excessive. Indeed, in one study of online shoppers, 56% said they would abandon a shopping cart if the delivery charges were too high; 68% of online shoppers in the same study said that their number one recommendation for online retailers would be to provide free shipping.[4] This should come as no surprise: when you buy something from a real-world shop there is no charge for delivery of the item to the store. We are not used to paying extra to receive goods; instead, our normal way of thinking is that the price of the item includes everything. Many online retailers make it doubly hard on themselves by hiding such additional costs until the last minute, causing millions of people to stop buying.

Free shipping comes at a cost

Of course, free shipping is not actually free. Take Amazon, which provides "free shipping" to its Prime members. That involves an annual cost of £49 in the UK or $79 in the US. Nevertheless, as long as you order more than about 16 items a year from Amazon, you will save money; if you order more than that, the shipping on those additional items will effectively be free. On top of this, the Prime service also provides guaranteed next-day delivery in the UK (within two days in the US) and the ability to borrow books for your Kindle if you have one, instead of buying them; US members get unlimited streaming of movies and television programs through Prime Instant Video as well. So for many people the subscription pays for itself several times over. The benefit for Amazon is that the service locks in customers who will prefer to shop on Amazon so they don't face unexpected shipping costs. With sales of more than £1,500 per second, even the smallest reduction in shopping cart abandonment can have a significant impact.

Online fashion retailer Asos has followed a similar path with its Premier service. For £9.95 a year you get unlimited next-day delivery without a minimum order value, as well as a fashion magazine subscription that normally retails for £14.95. What is surprising is that so few other online retailers have adopted this kind of approach.

What many companies do instead is offer free shipping as standard if your shopping basket is over a certain total. For example, the online Lego store expects you to spend a minimum of $99 before you get shipping free of charge. Other US stores only offer free shipping on one day each year, the Monday before Christmas, which has been labeled "Free Shipping Day" since 2009.

The vast majority of stores could do well to take on board that the word "free" is a powerful emotional trigger. In his book *Predictably Irrational*, behavioral economist Dan Ariely detailed experiments that showed that people are attracted by the concept of free.[5] If online shops were to highlight "free" shipping much more than they do, not only would they reduce the extent to which customers give up shopping because of the additional fees, people would actually be more likely to want to shop with them in the first place.

Slowness causes frustration

Another issue that puts people off buying online is that the website itself is just slow. According to one study, simply speeding up the shopping cart pages can increase sales by two-thirds.[6]

This issue gets ever more obvious as the speed of broadband increases. Already several million people in the UK, for example, have very high-speed broadband access of 60 Mbps or more, which enables websites to appear instantly without any noticeable delay. If an online retailer cannot present the shopping cart information in the blink of an eye, those with rapid broadband get annoyed because they are not used to waiting. And even if you have an average broadband speed, waiting for more than a couple of seconds is still frustrating.

Online shops blame the load on their servers, the size of their database, and a host of other issues. But in reality they are failing to invest in the technology needed to satisfy customer demand. And that means they are losing out. Shoppers don't give them the benefit of the doubt; instead, they move on to a site that can load the shopping cart more quickly.

Several studies have been conducted that demonstrate the urgent need for online shops to improve the speed of their websites dramatically. WordStream, an online advertising and marketing consultancy, found that by improving the load time for its website there was a 15% increase in conversion rates.[7] This example is confirmed with evidence from KissMetrics, a company that specializes in helping online businesses retain customers. KissMetrics established that a one-second delay in a web page loading could reduce sales conversions by 7%.[8] In addition, it discovered that if a sales page loads slowly, 79% of people would not return to that site to buy again in the future.

Research conducted by QuBit, an online data consultancy, predicted that latency (slow-loading shopping carts and sales pages) could have cost the online economy a massive £4.08bn by the end of 2013.[9] It noted that some online retailers, such as furniture giant IKEA, were doing well with the speed of their systems, but others, such as the bookstore Barnes & Noble, were faring badly in terms of load times – a massive 11 times slower than IKEA at the time of the research in March 2012. Interestingly, IKEA's online sales for 2011–12 increased by almost 25%, whereas Barnes & Noble's online sales decreased over the year.

Slow websites also make frequent mistakes: data entered into a form is not there when the page refreshes, for instance, so it has to be entered all over again. Many online shops fail to keep information from one screen in the shopping cart to the next, which means customers get annoyed and exasperated, and again are far less likely to proceed or return.

What if people want to think about their purchase?

Online shoppers are well informed and know how to hunt for a bargain. So they will often go to a shop, fill up their basket, and then head off to a competing store to do the same. Then they can compare the total costs, including taxes and delivery charges, and see when their items will be delivered. At that point, they can confirm one shopping basket and empty the other one. However, to do this they have to be able to save the shopping cart so they can come back to it later.

In the real world, you do this all the time. You wander around a shop, look at some items, and mentally earmark them for purchase. Then you go and have a coffee and a think, come back to the shop, go straight to the items you want, and take them to the checkout. Some real-world shops will even put items aside until you've made up your mind.

Yet online, many retailers won't let you save your shopping cart, meaning you either have to buy now, or go through the whole palaver again when you've finally decided you do want to buy. Not being able to save the shopping cart for later use is the cause of around one in four carts being abandoned.

Sometimes, of course, you don't get the opportunity to save things because you get distracted by something else, or mistakenly close a browser window when you didn't mean to. Some shopping cart systems provide a way around this. Shopify provides the details of your shopping history to the owner of the shop and gives them the opportunity to email you a link to re-create your shopping basket. This helps its users reduce the impact of shopping cart abandonment on their overall sales, but it also helps customers if they do want to come back to the purchase later. ShopFactory offers similar software.

There are two main systems in use: a persistent shopping cart and a perpetual shopping cart. A persistent shopping cart is the kind used by Shopify and large retailers such as Amazon. It remembers what you wanted to buy even if you log out of the store or close the browser window. Most stores do this by setting a "cookie," a small text file that is stored on your computer; when you go back to the shop at a later date, it looks to see whether you have that cookie and if you do it copies the information from it into the shopping cart.

A perpetual shopping cart is different. It is always present, usually along the top of the browser window. As you go from page to page it keeps a running total of any items you decide to buy. According to one study, online retailers prefer this kind of shopping cart because it helps increase sales conversion rates: people know what they have spent already and can keep within their budget.[10] It also often means that if you leave the store and come back later, your shopping is saved and you don't have to start again. However, not all perpetual carts allow you to save your shopping for subsequent purchase – they expect you to check out now. This can frustrate customers who think they have stored their shopping when in fact they have only done so for a short period. The real issue is the lack of consistency.

The problem of saving your shopping for later consideration is exacerbated by the fact that people may start their online shopping while on their desktop computer in their office, only to finish it on their smartphone on the way home. If the shop does not use a persistent cart, people will have to start their shopping all over again. Luckily, a relatively new player in the shopping cart arena, Magento, is fast becoming a standard for many online stores. It is focused on providing a consistent shopping experience across a range of devices by using a persistent cart mechanism.

It's a taxing moment

Another reason people give up on shopping carts is the discovery that tax such as VAT has to be paid. Rather like the shipping charge, many online retailers leave this to the last minute. In the EU, the situation is not helped by laws that apply differently online and offline. For instance, if you buy a book in a bricks-and-mortar bookshop in the UK you pay no VAT, but if you buy the same book for an ebook reader, such as the Kindle, it does attract VAT. Amazon is clear that the price you see is the price you pay, but other online retailers are not so accommodating.

In the US this area could become extremely complicated if the Marketplace Fairness Act were to be passed, which would require sales tax to be paid on online purchases, although the legislation is still currently being debated.

Making people spend more than they want

Several online retailers use the shopping cart process to tempt people into buying more than they had originally set out to do. They call this "upselling" or "cross-selling" – they tempt people into buying something extra to go with what they have just put in the cart, or they suggest other items that are similar. Many bricks-and-mortar stores do the same: you get to the checkout to pay for your goods when the sales assistant points out "today's special offers." McDonald's famously upsells its burgers with the "Would you like fries with that?" suggestion.

In McDonald's the upsell happens before you are in paying mode, while you are deciding what to buy. But online these upsells often occur after you've decided what to buy, and they are annoying because at that stage you have finished making your selection. In particular, people don't like what are referred to as "spammy" upsells, when the shopping cart automatically adds something extra that the shop thinks they will like. It adds only a few dollars to the total charge, but if the shop manages to get away with that several thousand times it becomes a nice little earner.

Nevertheless, some online stores clearly do understand upselling, cross-selling, and making the shopping cart experience work well. Once again, Amazon is a good example.

CASE STUDY: THE 1-CLICK SYSTEM

Only Amazon and Apple (which licenses the technology from Amazon) have a shopping cart capable of allowing people to buy in a single click. Even though it was disputed when it was first applied for, the Amazon patent for its trademarked "1-Click" shopping cart means the company has the exclusive rights on the technology until 2017. Essentially, this system removes all of those inconveniences of online shopping carts. You don't have to fill in forms each time you buy anything or confirm any personal details. You just select the item you want, confirm the addressee, press the 1-Click button, and you've bought it.

Amazon is also fastidious with the data it collects about its customers. In an interview with *Forbes* magazine, the company's founder Jeff Bezos explained that it has a "culture of metrics" whereby every ounce of information about customer behavior is measured and analyzed.[11] As a result, Amazon can provide useful and interesting upsells and cross-sells with "Customers who bought this item also bought" kinds of offers, or "New for you." The upsell takes place before the final act of pressing the "Proceed to Checkout" button, meaning that the promotion of additional items is much less irritating than with many other shopping carts.

In a thorough review the Rejoiner website, which specializes in converting prospects into buyers online, pointed out that Amazon's shopping cart was cut down to the basics, which is potentially one of the reasons it is the number one online consumer shop in the world.[12]

Do you want people to buy?

Even if an online store has managed to organize its shopping cart as well as Amazon, many still don't encourage people to buy. In fact, only 13% of companies ever contact a customer again if they fill up a shopping cart and then give up. That's rather like someone walking up to the till in a physical shop, handing over what they want to buy, then walking away and the shop assistant not saying a word to them. In the real world they'd at least ask the person whether they were OK and the assistant may even come running after them. But in the online world, the vast majority of retailers carry on as though nothing has happened.

Shoppers like to feel that they are wanted, that their custom is welcomed, but in essence, not emailing someone to say "Did you mean to finish your shopping?" is a signal that the retailer doesn't care about them or doesn't "like" them.

And think about what happens *after* the customer has bought something and finished the shopping cart process. Have them land on a page that thanks them for their custom, to make them feel appreciated, and maybe offer a code for a little something extra on their next visit to encourage repeat business. Also, ensure that your system emails a receipt for every purchase. Sometimes online shopping can feel like going into a black hole at the end, so hold people's hand with attentive customer service and ensure the email tells them whom to contact if they have any questions.

The perfect shopping cart

There is plenty of advice to businesses online about constructing the perfect shopping cart to avoid abandonment or reducing the rate at which shoppers give up buying at the last moment. Few online retailers seem to heed the advice, even though the steps required are remarkably simple. What online retailers need to do is:

- ◆ Provide a clean, simple, uncluttered shopping and payment system.
- ◆ Offer free shipping and delivery – or at least announce the charges before people start shopping.
- ◆ Show tax-inclusive pricing.
- ◆ Allow all forms of payment.
- ◆ Avoid spammy upsells.
- ◆ Make sure that the website is fast and maintains form data from screen to screen.
- ◆ Ensure that the shopping cart is mobile friendly.
- ◆ Show customers that they are wanted if for any reason they leave the website during a transaction.

BLUEPRINT

Choosing the right shopping cart technology is essential. You will definitely lose sales if your shopping cart does not work well and if it does not work on mobiles and tablets.

1. Make sure that people can check out in the fewest possible clicks. One click is not possible as that is patented by Amazon, but two clicks should be achievable.
2. Make sure that your shopping cart is mobile friendly.
3. Always have a shopping cart logo visible on the top of each page, as well as the number of items in the cart. People often move around a website and lose their way back to the checkout.
4. Collect as little data as necessary: too many boxes on forms reduce sales.
5. Ensure that your shopping cart is VAT-ready if you're selling to Europe. Several popular shopping cart programs are inadequate when it comes to handling taxes, VAT, and invoicing.
6. Do not add surprise extra costs at the checkout. Keep your customers informed of what they can expect to pay.
7. Make sure that your shopping cart system provides email receipts to buyers.

6

HAPPY CUSTOMERS BUY AGAIN

In the world of online retail, customers expect much higher levels of customer service than have traditionally been accepted in the offline world. This is partly because there has been widespread publicity for companies that offer exceptional service, which makes people realize what is possible and raises their expectations as a result.

Most retailers, on- or offline, could learn a lot from online shoe and fashion store Zappos. It describes itself as a customer service business that happens to sell things. Now owned by Amazon but run largely independently, Zappos has 10 core values, none of which has anything to do with sales. In its first six years of business, it went from nothing to almost $1bn of sales – with no focus on selling. Instead, it focuses on retaining customers through providing them with such fantastic service they will not want to shop anywhere else. Examples of the lengths to which Zappos goes include providing a pair of shoes for a wedding guest who had forgotten them, sending flowers to a woman who had sore feet, and never reading from any kind of customer service script. The result is that 75% of their customers are repeat buyers and most of the company's marketing is by word of mouth only.

On the Zappos.com website, there is a clear link to a returns section, which appears at the top right of every page of the site. This provides clear instructions together with an additional two pages of in-depth detail on how to send your items back. Furthermore, the pages explain that you can return any item up to 365 days after buying it. That's right – a full year after buying from Zappos you can still send something back. In fact, if you happen to buy on February 29 in a leap year, you have four years to change your mind, because the anniversary of the day you bought it doesn't arise until then. Not only that, returns are free: all a customer has to do is take the box back to a UPS outlet or a post office, which means it is convenient no matter where you live.

You might think this is crazy. Rather than trying to hide away the ability to send items back, Zappos positively encourages customers to over-order and return what they don't want. To do so it has to absorb huge costs, not only in the shipping charges both ways but in extra stock to allow for over-ordering. Nevertheless, it believes this is worth the extra investment because it is a company to which customer service is paramount.

Zappos' CEO Tony Hsieh told *Success* magazine:

> *The year 2007 was the first where we made a significant profit. It was roughly 5 percent operating margins off of our net sales. Several years prior to that, we ran the company at break-even in order to maximize our growth. We could have made a profit in any of the previous three years, but we decided, whatever profit we did make, to reinvest it back into the business.*[1]

The high costs of the operation and the ease of returns appear to be profitable, and indeed Amazon has kept Zappos as a separate brand, not integrating it within the main store.

An indicator of the importance of excellent customer service was revealed in a 2011 *Financial Times* article about Zappos.[2] In the first few years of its existence, the company used the drop-ship method of working: it took orders and sent them direct to the suppliers of shoes, who then fulfilled the orders to the customers. However, the shoe companies frequently failed to deliver on time, or at all. This meant that Zappos had to resort to stocking and distributing shoes itself, in order to meet its stated levels of customer service.

Zappos was not the first online retailer to have to do this. Amazon also began as a drop-ship firm, but later had to invest in warehousing and distribution in order to provide a good customer experience. A key promise of the internet – to enable retailers to operate without the need for stock – failed to materialize because of poor service from traditional industries.

You don't have to be a behemoth like Amazon to provide high levels of service straightaway, however, as the example of Bellabox illustrates.

CASE STUDY: BELLABOX

The Singaporean beauty and cosmetics firm Bellabox has a free returns policy that is clearly explained on its website. The returns options are clearly marked from each page and there is a simple FAQ system for answering questions about returns.

In essence, the policy states that shoppers can return anything within seven days of receipt and that Bellabox will bear the cost of the return shipping. There is an email address to contact where the return can be arranged.

While these terms may not be as generous as those offered by Zappos, for a relatively small company they are very good indeed.

Of course, even though customer expectations online may well be free returns, this may be unprofitable for some retailers. Therefore striking the right balance between what the customers want and what can be achieved profitably is important. A clue to the approach

you need to take is provided by Chinese research conducted at
Nankai University.[3] This found that customer expectations in relation to returns were linked to product quality and price. The higher
the price and the greater the quality, the more you need to have
free returns; low-cost, low-quality items do not necessarily require
such a policy.

The customer is always wrong

A further aspect of customer service is providing help and information to customers about the products they buy. Recently, however,
one of the biggest money-saving changes for manufacturers has
been the removal of printed manuals from many products. Instead,
you may receive a leaflet saying you can go to a website to download a PDF. This saves on printing costs as well as shipping, as the
weight of the package is reduced. Furthermore, companies can extol
their "green" credentials, because they are saving paper as well as
reducing the load on transportation and therefore generating fewer

greenhouse gases. On top of this, they can provide several different language versions of manuals on their website, thus increasing customer satisfaction. So what is there not to like about PDF manuals?

Quite a lot, if you read online forums and blogs. Complaints are rife about the lack of printed manuals in product boxes. One thread in the Digital Photography Review forum, for instance, ran from December 2010 to July 2011 complaining about the lack of a printed manual for the Canon SX30 camera.[4] As the complainers pointed out, having a manual on a CD or a website does not really help a photographer who is out taking photographs, away from a computer or phone signal, whereas a printed manual can easily be slipped into a camera bag.

In a BBC Radio 4 documentary about manuals, Dr. Mark Miodownik from King's College, London said that printed manuals represent a link between the product and the user.[5] Without a manual, the product is more isolated from its owner, who may have less of a connection with the brand.

There is also a hidden cost for manufacturers: the need for more customer service staff to handle calls and emails from people who cannot find the answer to their question. Performance in most customer call centers is measured on the time taken to deal with calls, with constant pressure on staff to take the lowest amount of time possible. (Compare that with Zappos, where one call lasted an astonishing 10 hour 29 minutes; the company focuses on quality, not time.) One of the most widely used acronyms in customer call centers is RTFM, standing for "Read The Flipping Manual" (I've toned down the actual wording). But if there is no manual, customer service staff have to repeat information on a seemingly endless basis, making them frustrated and potentially having a negative effect on service.

According to the Customer Experience Impact Report from RightNow.com, 82% of people will not return to a store if they have a bad experience.[6] Furthermore, 66% of customers said they would spend more if they had a good experience and that customer service is the main reason for people recommending a particular company, ahead of the products themselves. In other words, good customer service can raise your income and gain you more customers. Yet money-saving measures like removing printed manuals only serve to increase customers' dissatisfaction, reducing their feelings of good service.

Help me, I'm lost

My 13-year-old son Elliot recently went on an exchange trip to France, spending a fortnight with a French family. A few weeks before he left I bought him a new mobile phone from Tesco Mobile. It was a great deal: the smartphone he wanted on an affordable monthly contract. However, I was concerned after a day or two when we had not heard from him. Eventually, he phoned using the French family's landline to say that even though his phone was working and could receive calls or text messages, he could not make any calls. It seemed as though it was an inbound-only phone. So I went to the Tesco Mobile website, where I found a help section and a section about using your phone abroad. As I started to read, a small window popped up asking me if I would like a chat.

So I typed in my problem and pressed "Chat now." Within seconds, I had a typed message back from a customer service agent who asked me for some more details about the issue. He politely asked me to wait a moment or two while he checked a few things. Then he told me what the issue was and how to solve it. One minute later, my son's phone was working in France and he sent me a "thank-you" text message. The problem was one I could have worked out myself from the help files on the website, if I had gone through them carefully, but that would have taken a longer time. The chat facility worked like a dream in guiding me to the quickest solution.

Research from customer service software company Synthetix shows that more people now go to the web to get help and support than pick up the telephone.[7] Indeed, Synthetix points out that the internet is the number one place where people expect retailers to provide support and customer service options. However, importantly, the study also reveals that such assistance needs to be speedy.

For online retailers this means that customer service options should focus on the website first, with all other areas of support, such as telephone advice, being secondary. The customer service center on your website needs to be the hub from which all other aspects of customer support derive. A good example of this is provided by Australian discount department store Big W. It was inspected by the "mystery shopping" team from Choice.com, who found the store to be providing excellent levels of service. However, not all customers can visit the company's bricks-and-mortar stores for advice, so it has a comprehensive online system of help and support. Its website includes a comprehensive and well-designed FAQ system clearly categorized in several different areas. The website also features a visible telephone number and a contact section allowing the customer to dictate how they want a reply – whether they would like someone to phone them back, for instance. This well-put-together system of online support for customers is a clear example of what can be done effectively online.

> TIP: Monitor the most frequent issues your customers have and establish a comprehensive Frequently Asked Questions (FAQ) section for your online help center.

The speed with which people can access information online, the change in attention spans, and the cultural shift toward instant gratification all mean that people are becoming increasingly impatient with retailers who cannot deal with product questions or support problems right now, this minute. In fact, the study by RightNow.com found that 2 in every 100 customers wanted a response to their issue within 60 seconds. Most people were not that fussy, but 42% of people did expect a same-day response. Moreover, social customer service company Conversocial found that 81% of people using Twitter expected a same-day response to any communication they had with a company. Those who use Twitter are accustomed to rapid-fire conversations and expect the same from the companies they contact. However, analytics company Simply Measured found that many firms were failing to live up to customers' speed requirements, reporting a study in which no firms were achieving a response within 30 minutes. Even if customers wanted a reply within an hour, only 9% of firms were able to realize this, although all of the companies were capable of dealing with customer issues in a "few days." Companies are still not geared up to the speed customers require when they need help, handholding, or have any kind of question that needs to be answered.

> Surveys show that most online stores are way behind customer expectations in terms of service and support. Some 80% of companies believe they provide superior support, but only 8% of customers think that. There is a gulf to bridge.

Surprising people makes them like you

At 7.30 p.m. on December 24, 2011, the 173 passengers on board Spanair Flight JK6474 from Barcelona to A Coruña on the northwest coast of Spain had no idea what was about to happen. They were on their way home for Christmas, but midway through their flight they heard an announcement that they will probably remember for the rest of their lives. The cabin steward told them they had just flown past Father Christmas on his trip around the world. And by some mid-air magic, he had been able to deliver presents to all the children on board. The entire story is shown on YouTube, of course.[8]

This is an example of a random act of kindness, doing something completely unexpected for your customers. Sadly for Spanair, it came too late to save the company from going into administration at the beginning of 2012 following a failed takeover bid. Nevertheless, other companies have performed similar acts and lived to tell the tale. For instance, flower delivery network Interflora set up a Twitter campaign in 2012 looking for people in the UK who needed cheering up. Once it had identified them because of a miserable tweet they had written, the company contacted them, obtained their home address, and sent round a bunch of flowers.

Meanwhile, in America, a customer service call at the cloud services company Rackspace was taking some time and the company employee heard the customer say, in the background, that they were hungry. So while continuing to talk to the client, the Rackspace employee ordered some takeaway food and had it sent to the customer, who was still on the phone when the doorbell rang. The customer service agent simply told them to answer the door because it would be a free pizza.

This kind of action has been tested in psychological research and been shown to help, but only if people do *not* expect to get something from you. Researchers from Monmouth University, New Jersey found that when chocolate was provided along with the bill in a restaurant, tips were proportional to the amount of chocolate.[9] This "reciprocity effect" occurs when people are given something unexpectedly, which makes them feel good so they respond in kind.

For online retailers, this can mean rewarding people with unexpected gifts in their delivery parcel. For example, I recently ordered some sports clothing for my son on the Sports Direct website. He was delighted when he also received a Sports Direct mug as a gift.

Automation fails to help retailers

When business owners are asked what they expect the internet to do for them, the number one answer is always "save money." The web can save your business money, of course, but it can also increase your spending. Business leaders often ignore the fact that while many processes can be streamlined, such as updating accounts software immediately with actual sales, online business itself can create a completely new array of processes that require managing, thereby increasing costs. These include managing links on various websites, ensuring the website has correct prices displayed, and keeping in touch with customers. However, the mental focus on cost saving frequently leads online retailers to automate as many of their systems as possible.

One of the most common automations is the email "sequential autoresponder." You will be familiar with autoresponders that send out a message when someone is on holiday or away from their desk. A sequential autoresponder is similar, but it sends out multiple messages over a long period. Many retailers add you to an autoresponder series the moment you order something from their website. The first message thanks you for your order and provides you with useful information, such as links to support pages. A few days later, you might receive a second message, just checking that everything is OK and reminding you of the company's phone number in case you need to call. So far, so useful. A week later, you get another email saying that because you bought that item recently, you might be interested in products that complement it. And so it goes, on and on until you unsubscribe.

There are plenty of definitions of spam, but there is only one definition to which online retailers should adhere: if a customer thinks something is spam, it is spam. Even if they signed up to receive your emails by ticking an "I agree" box, if they get annoyed, you're sending them spam.

That is not the only problem with emails. Research by email marketing company MailChimp showed that only 34% of emails sent by retail outlets are actually opened. This is typical for many industries; indeed some, like daily deals, have much lower opening rates. In addition the bounce rate – the percentage of email messages that are not delivered – is low for the retail sector, presumably because an accurate address is required to receive the goods you order. Even so, more than two-thirds of shoppers who have signed up to receive marketing emails fail to actually receive them. Many of them could well have automated their removal straight to the trash. All of the major email programs, such as Gmail and Microsoft Outlook, have filters that enable this, and a simple search on Google will find a plethora of articles explaining how to filter out unwanted mail. Whatever the reason for emails not being read, it is not good news for retailers.

TIP: Relying on autoresponders to market your online shop can create a negative customer response. Use the facility with care and create emails that people want to read.

The other issue with automated emails is a lack of personalization to the individual shopper. Many online shops appear to believe that simply by writing to someone using their first name, they have personalized the email. This is not personalization, merely correct addressing.

At the beginning of 2013, consultancy firm Ovum pointed out that several technologies are combining to help people get completely personalized services. Yet at the same time, industries such as insurance are moving toward "one-to-many" messaging through mass media. Google personalizes search results based on knowledge of each individual searcher's habits; Amazon personalizes its pages for each customer depending on their searches and buying patterns; Facebook is also personalized to individual likes and dislikes. Thus customers' online experience is of deep personalization, and if retailers do not provide this, they are not matching customer expectations. That implies that in relation to the automated aspects of an online store, far greater levels of personalization need to be built in, or more activities need to be done manually, by real people.

Talking is good

In order to personalize the experience your customers receive, you need to know a great deal about them. So it makes sense to collect as much information as possible about your online customers when they buy from you or at other points in the relationship, such as on Facebook or in a real-world store. However, customers can be resistant to giving out too much information online.

The main issue is that people are concerned about security and privacy, which makes them wary of providing too many personal details. One of the key psychological functions of privacy is autonomy, being in charge of our lives and not having other people interfere. Nevertheless, according to the *Oxford Handbook of Internet Psychology*, people are prepared to trade privacy for convenience if they know they can gain some benefits from releasing certain personal information.[10] Herein lies the problem for internet retailers: if you are to gain more information from customers so that you can be more personal, you are going to have to inconvenience them by getting them to give you those details.

Research by Eloqua, a customer experience software company that is part of Oracle, shows that the more fields there are on a web form, the fewer people engage with it. The study demonstrates a reasonably straight-line relationship between the total number of fields and the conversion rate: fewer fields equal higher conversions.[11] Yet as already stressed, understanding customers is fundamental to delivering the increased levels of personalization that people require.

According to Jaynie L. Smith, CEO of US firm Smart Advantage and a leading international expert on competitive advantage, few businesses really understand their customers in any meaningful way. Indeed, in her book *Relevant Selling*, she claims that companies offer what they think their customers want, which is often wide of the mark in terms of what they really want.[12] For instance, many retailers believe they know what their customers want to buy, focusing their thinking on "what" is on sale. However, studies show that customers know they can buy most things from a variety of stores, so what they are actually looking for is "how" a company sells the products, such as the degree of customer care.

The problem is that the internet gives companies the illusion that they understand their customers. It provides them with "big data" – lots of information about customer activities online. It draws heat maps to visualize where on their site customers click and it offers many other ways to track what people do on web pages. It shows what they type into search boxes, where they go, and where they come from. Retailers are not in the least short of information about their online customers, except for one thing: they no longer glean information by being in the presence of another human being. The internet lacks the ability to interpret body language or tone of voice, and it doesn't allow online retailers to make an impression at a subconscious level by chatting to customers. For all its data, the internet is superficial compared with the subconscious power of human beings.

In bricks-and-mortar stores, sales staff "know" their regular customers; indeed, they can often relate interesting stories and tidbits about them. In addition, they know what kind of mood a customer is in when they walk into the store because of their facial expression, their gait, or even the clothes they have chosen to wear. All of this information is used to help strengthen relationships with customers. Try doing that online.

One of the most important things online retailers need to do to improve their level of customer service is to understand their customers on a human level, and one of the most effective ways of doing that is to talk to them.

> TIP: Speak to your customers more. Phone them, hold events, socialize with them, and get to know them. That's what successful firms did prior to the internet, and you need to find ways to continue the habit.

Big or small, it doesn't matter

Whether you are a big business or you run a small retailer is immaterial to the shopper. They do not care if you are small and cannot afford sufficient staff to answer the phone "instantly." Neither do they care if you are such a big online retailer that getting close to your customers and talking to them on a regular basis is nearly impossible. All the customer really cares about is good service.

Essentially, the most consistent finding in research about customer service is that people simply want you to show that you do care, that it is your actions that matter more than your words. Your website can repeat all kinds of platitudes suggesting you care for your customers, but unless people can see it or feel it you may as well not have those web pages in place.

Whether you are big or small customers want you to answer their emails quickly, they want the ability to speak to someone on the phone who actually understands their problems and they want to feel as though they are being listened to. In a small retailer, for instance, this could mean that every member of staff answers the phone and is empowered to deal with any customer issue. In a large retailer it might mean that you have regular focus groups where you meet customers face to face. Such activities are not major budgetary problems. Largely they are a matter of attitude. Good customer service can be achieved on a small budget if you have the right attitude, placing your relationship with your customers at the center of the business. Zappos is a large global business that achieves stunning customer service by ensuring that everyone it employs has the right attitude to customers. But the example of Bellabox also demonstrates that smaller businesses can achieve high levels of service when they focus their activity on pleasing the customer.

BLUEPRINT

There is little to distinguish between many stores online. The products you sell can probably be bought in many other shops, unless you are truly niche in your approach. So the only real way online stores can differentiate themselves is through excellent customer service.

1. Make customer service central to your business, not merely an add-on.
2. Create an online customer service, support, and help center on the web, even if you have a mainly offline business.
3. Produce a customer service policy and returns policy and make these highly visible on your website.
4. Set up a system so you can respond to customer queries as rapidly as possible, preferably within an hour.
5. Consider using live chat facilities to appeal to the customer's need for speed.
6. If possible, provide free returns, at the customer's convenience.
7. Surprise your customers in altruistic ways.
8. Increase the level of personalization in your business substantially, especially in email marketing.
9. Meet your customers in the real world whenever possible. Failing that, speak to them on the telephone. Get to know them and they will want to maintain a relationship with you.

7
DO MY FRIENDS LIKE IT?

Channel 4 Television in the UK has a daily program that is addictive to watch. *Come Dine with Me* is a "reality" program in which members of the public compete to hold the best dinner party at their home. Each night, one of the contestants hosts a dinner party and their guests mark them out of ten. Over four or five days, the contestants have eaten several meals, been to each other's houses, and rated everyone's cooking and entertainment skills. The winner gets a cool £1,000 in cash.

As a psychologist, it is interesting to watch the interactions taking place and observe the behavior of the people on the program. Each episode contains a vast amount of noise: chitchat, laughter, and comment, including about the host's home as well as their food. The program illustrates the fact that when you put a group of people together they cannot help themselves – they have to compete, share their ideas, and offer their views. Human beings are preprogrammed to be social; it *is* human nature.

Part of the reason we love to talk is to help us create our identity. What we say to people assists in confirming our views, and the things people say to us combine to create our internal picture of ourselves. Conversation is what helps us feel "whole." Socializing also gives us a sense of belonging, either to a physical group or to some kind of affiliation. As a result, it contributes to building self-esteem. Socializing also has purposes for society, ensuring that we all get along together, that groups function, and that we can achieve success overall. Indeed, without the ability to socialize and get on with each other we would not be able to reproduce or bring up our young. Our brains have social activity hard-wired into them.

It is therefore little wonder that Facebook has become such a phenomenon. Half the people who use the internet are members of Facebook and over 650 million log in every day. On average, every person who uses Facebook is spending 22 minutes on it every day, far longer than on any other single website. And overall, social networking accounts for 27% of all our internet activity. It functions as an extension of our desire, need, and in-built attraction to be social.

Widespread social networking carries an important implication for retailers. Because this is the most common way people now use the internet, social networking sites frame expectations of how other sites should function. If your online store does not operate in some social way, such as by allowing people to share their purchases and so tapping into their desire to be liked, then you are not delivering what your customers want. This mismatch to expectations may cause you to lose business.

> **Social networking sites frame people's expectations of how other websites should work.**

Sharing comes naturally to shoppers

Being social may well be natural, but you might think sharing is not such a great idea. After all, if we share things we reduce our chances of competing and winning, of attaining self-actualization, as described in American psychologist Abraham Maslow's "Hierarchy of Needs." However, sharing turns out to be a basic element of our brain. When we were evolving and food supplies were scarce, sharing helped to even out the available resources, enhancing group survival. Sharing also prevents one group becoming dominant, a further essential component in survival. And studies of primates show that sharing is one of the ways that leads to sex. Hence sharing is a natural behavior in many species.

In a groundbreaking study in 2011 by the *New York Times'* Customer Insight Group, one of the participants revealed that the concept of sharing was nothing new to her: she and her friends had been sharing what they had bought for years, over dinners or at coffee meetings.[1] The research revealed that people like to share because:

◆ It makes them feel more involved with the world around them.
◆ It makes them feel valued.
◆ It helps them maintain social connections that would otherwise be lost.
◆ It allows them to demonstrate support for specific things.

These researchers claim to have identified six types of sharers online, ranging from those who share merely to help others, to individuals who share mainly to enhance their career or stir up discussion. In reality, though, it is more likely that people share in different ways according to the circumstances. What is important for retailers is to know what it is they should provide that people would want to share.

This is where the *New York Times* study makes a particularly important finding: the things that people share the most are those that help them connect to each other. Merely saying "I have just bought this" has no value unless doing so connects you with other people, such as by "I have bought this" appearing on your friends' Facebook timelines. Otherwise it is mere bragging.

> TIP: Encourage your shoppers to share their purchases. It will help them feel good about you, as well as create increased awareness of your store.

One other aspect of sharing worthy of consideration is novelty. Human beings have another rather basic instinct, present in our brains from our evolutionary beginnings. We tend to keep our attention ready to pounce at a moment's notice on something new and different. We prefer new things to old because in our early days as human beings we learned that fresh, new food was much more likely to help us survive than old, rotting food. We are primed to be attracted to the novel because it boosts survival. As a result, people prefer to share something new, different, and unusual. If an online shop can provide interesting products for customers to share, so much the better.

A further element of sharing is personal – for the sharer, not for the recipient of what is being shared – and that is emotional arousal. We tend to share most when we can emotionally connect with our real friends. We also share when other emotions are triggered, such as happiness, sadness, anger, or even erotic feelings. One of the emotions that leads to the greatest degree of sharing is humor; funny videos are among the most widely shared items on YouTube, for instance.

Before we look at some individual social media sites, there are some principles to follow if you want material from your online shop to be shared:

◆ Make your content emotionally arousing – people mostly share things that make them feel happy.
◆ Make your content novel and different – people are not interested in the "same old," it has to be different or new.
◆ Make your content help people connect with others – people are mostly interested in sharing if they can do so with their friends and not the world in general.

When you fulfill those three criteria, the natural sharing instincts of your customers will kick in and your store will gain additional word-of-mouth exposure.

TIP: Consider adding easy-to-use sharing software such as justbought.it to enable your customers to share what they have bought from your site.

Facebook is a shopper's dream

It is undeniable that Facebook is a phenomenon. People spend more time, on average, on Facebook than on any other website – so much so that psychologists are treating cases of "Facebook addiction." However, in addition to the obvious chatting and connecting with friends it allows us to do, several features of the site are very good for shoppers.

Many shops or brands have Facebook pages, which shoppers can visit for the latest information or gossip about the company.

They can see pictures of events and they can leave messages of support. This is all part of helping people build their personal identity and making them feel part of the "tribe." However, one key issue is that people feel isolated if they are one of only a few contributing to a page, or if they get no response. Consequently, online retailers with Facebook pages need to make sure that there are regular contributions, that they "seed" the page with items for discussion, and that they respond when their customers say something. Otherwise, customers can feel neglected and ignored, and form a negative association with the shop.

One company that uses Facebook well is American department store Target. It posts regularly, holds conversations with customers, and clearly employs the site as a tool for engagement. In addition, it holds regular promotions, giving discounts and special offers exclusively to people who "Like" its page. This is an important psychological factor because it makes its followers feel like "VIPs," different from others who shop at Target but don't follow it on Facebook.

To enable shoppers to share their purchases with their friends, retailers should have links on their web pages to their Facebook page, as well as links on email receipts and "order completed" pages so people can immediately share what they have bought.

> TIP: Only use Facebook to engage with your customers if you are prepared to respond regularly and post fresh content daily at the very least.

Twitter is a complainer's dream

If you monitor Facebook to engage with your customers, then you absolutely have to monitor Twitter as well. The main reason behind saying this is to do with what people are likely to tweet – complaints. Twitter provides people who have a grievance with a perfect tool for getting it off their chest.

Of course, people have always complained. The first research that explained why was from the University of Florida, several years before the invention of Twitter.[2] This study found that people mostly complain to receive feedback from their social group that their complaint is justified. In other words, most people who complain are not doing so for any kind of recompense, but to confirm to themselves that they were right all along.

So is it any wonder that Twitter is a highly popular place to complain about shops and our experiences with them? A few seconds spent typing in a complaint in 140 characters on Twitter and moments later we can get several followers saying "I agree" or "Well done" or some other confirmation that our views are correct.

The problem for retailers is that Twitter can easily inspire a sea of negativity. British fashion store Celeb Boutique had several complaints on Twitter following a public relations mess-up. The company had a dress on sale called "Aurora" and noticed on July 20, 2012 that "Aurora" was trending on Twitter, meaning thousands of people were using the word in their tweets. It sent this tweet as a result:

> #Aurora is trending, clearly about our Kim K inspired #Aurora
> dress

The problem was, the company had not investigated why the word "Aurora" was trending. In fact there had been a mass shooting at a cinema in the town of Aurora, Colorado. People were quick to take to Twitter and complain about Celeb Boutique, leading to a Facebook page being established to boycott the company. Celeb Boutique did respond, but it took an hour to delete the offensive tweet, allowing time for many more complaints to be posted.

In that example the initial context for sending the tweet was an innocent mistake, but other examples are rather more dubious. In October 2012, Hurricane Sandy was spreading its way up the east coast of America, inflicting damage across a wide area. Yet in spite of the death and destruction Sandy was causing, fashion store GAP sent out this tweet:

> All impacted by #Sandy, stay safe! We'll be doing lots of Gap.com
> shopping today. How about you?

Similarly, designer fashion label Kenneth Cole tweeted the following message during the "Arab Spring" uprisings in Egypt:

> *Millions in uproar in #Cairo. Rumor is they heard our new spring collection is now available online.*

That itself caused substantial uproar on Twitter. Such incidents provide several lessons for retailers. First, if people have a complaint they take to Twitter quickly, and if a complaint is made the matter has to be dealt with equally quickly to prevent further complaints and the whole thing spiraling out of control. That means retailers need to monitor Twitter on a continuous basis. As American online marketing expert David Meerman Scott says in his book *Real-Time Marketing and PR*, social media such as Twitter are merely the tools we use – what really needs to change is our mindset, so that we operate in "real time."[3]

People are being encouraged to complain via Twitter by other Twitter users and by media coverage of people who have achieved results by doing so, thus there is something of a self-reinforcing spiral here. Nevertheless, if you can respond quickly, your business can benefit. And remember that even if your business doesn't have its own Twitter account, people can still tweet about you by name or by using a hashtag in front – for instance #grahamjones – which is Twitter shorthand for a keyword and makes the word more easily searchable.

A good example is UK mobile telephone company O2, which suffered a major network outage in July 2012. The result was thousands of negative tweets that reached an estimated 1.7 million people. However, the company's response changed the sentiment of the Twittersphere, giving people plenty to smile about. For instance, one complaining tweet said that the individual had needed to travel to Italy to get a signal. The response from O2 was: "You can come back now, we're back in business." The responses weren't corporate but instead fun, "matey" kinds of tweets, which went a long way toward defusing the bad publicity created by the two-day outage.

TIP: To ensure that you are able to monitor Twitter for real-time complaints about your store, get a Twitter management tool such as HootSuite.

Nevertheless, Twitter can be difficult to use for overt marketing. People are wary of promotional tweets, even from companies they like. That's because unscrupulous online marketers have used Twitter to send out tweets that seem interesting, but when people click on the link it sends them to some kind of "buy it now" sales page, which was not what they were expecting and can annoy them. On Twitter, people are in conversation mode, not buying mode. Hence, promotional tweets that are purely designed to sell have little value.

A corollary of Twitter's potential to broadcast complaints is its potential to destroy trust. As we shall see in Chapter 8, trust is vital online. If your customers do not trust you, then you may as well give up.

The psychology of trust is complex, but the clearest explanation I ever heard was at a conference in Singapore. One of my fellow speakers was Dr. Vincent Covello, at that time from the University of Columbia, New York, who has specialized in understanding how trust and credibility are communicated in times of crisis. His research uncovered a fundamental component of communicating trust: showing that you care about the other person. His presentation was compelling and I reflected afterward that he had himself demonstrated absolute care for the needs of his conference audience. He walked the walk as well as talking the talk.

So the more you care for your customers, the more they trust you. Good customer service does much more than get people to say nice things about you: it helps ensure that they trust you. However, trust is an extremely fragile phenomenon. You only need to make one mistake and the bond can be broken. Therefore, anything that shows lack of care for the customer is likely to weaken trust – and this can be broadcast via Twitter.

Let me give you an illustration. In 2011, I took my son, then aged 11, to collect his grandfather, who had been on a coach trip. The appointed coach stop was a set of services on the motorway

not far from my home. It was around 5 p.m. on a Saturday evening
and when my father-in-law got off the coach he was hungry, as was
my son, so we went into the services to get a meal. Even though
it was a busy time, there was only one member of staff working
in the restaurant. Not only was he trying to serve meals, he was
supposed to pour drinks, take payment, and clear tables. As we
waited in line, I was getting somewhat frustrated by the delay and
noticed that the restaurant manager was standing nearby, watching
his member of staff trying to cope under the pressure.

"Could you serve?" I asked the manager.

He turned to me with a look of disdain, grunted, and then
walked straight through a door saying "Staff Only." Not only was
he failing to deal with the situation, he was also unwilling to help
or even demonstrate any care for his customers. It was as though
serving us was beneath him.

I took out my smartphone, logged onto Twitter, and sent out
a tweet, naming and shaming the company involved. My tweet
was retweeted, bringing it to the attention of potentially more than
100,000 people. My trust in the company had been broken, because
it did not care for my family or me, but now I had spread that
distrust to many other people who could well have second thoughts
about using the same company.

Pinterest is a retailer's dream

Pinterest is the social network that has had the most rapid rise to
fame. It was in beta testing for around three years before it officially
launched as an open, public site in August 2012. However, it grew
quickly even in beta, achieving 10 million users faster than any
other website. Today it has around 70 million users.

Different to Facebook and Twitter, which have a major text
element, Pinterest is all about sharing pictures. These can either be
images you have taken yourself or pictures you see on your trawls
around the web and that you simply like and want to share. This
sharing provides self-identity confirmation for users, but it also
offers a powerful opportunity to retailers.

Pinterest is easier for companies to use for promotional purposes. If you "pin" a product picture or something for sale, pricing information is included underneath the image. That means promotional pins are more easily identified and if someone is in buying mode and attracted by a product image, they are much less likely to react negatively when they click on the item.

As an example of what can be achieved, consider Ana White. Her shop sells products for "home makers." She has over 197,000 followers on Facebook, yet her number one source of referrals to her web store is Pinterest. She is selling highly visual items, such as furniture and design plans, which lend themselves to the entirely visual nature of the site.

TIP: If your products are visual, get them onto Pinterest to increase traffic to your online store.

Google+ is an expert's dream

Google+ is for geeks, particularly when compared to other social networks like Facebook. For a start, Google+ only had about one fifth of Facebook's number of users at the beginning of 2013. In an analysis of the world's Top 500 internet retailers, 473 of them were proud to display their Facebook Like button, whereas only 128 of them mentioned they were on Google+.[4]

However, the site does have some excellent features that are worthy of consideration by retailers. One is the concept of the Google Hangout. This provides free live video streaming and automatic recording to YouTube (also part of the behemoth Google, of course). This means that retailers could hold in-store demonstrations, extend them, free of charge, to the online world, and as a result have a video on YouTube that could be employed in further marketing initiatives.

Similarly, the Google+ concept of "circles" can be used to create VIP groupings of customers, giving them exclusive news about products or promotions. This would tap into that feeling of social exclusivity that increases consumers' connection to a company.

The problem is that few retailers are experimenting with Google+, and those that are appear to be focusing on its use for internal communication rather than connecting with customers. The Australian Dick Smith technology store chain, for instance, has started to use Google+ to share best practices between its 4,500 staff. That's a great idea, of course, but Google+ presents retailers with so many more options.

One in particular is an extension of the Dick Smith idea: sharing expertise. When it comes to high-value items, consumers like to believe they are buying from people who really know what they're talking about. Features such as Google Hangout provide retailers with the perfect opportunity to do this.

A social media strategy

Whether you use Google+, Pinterest, Twitter, or Facebook, one thing is for sure – you need to know *how* you are going to use each of these social networks. When I visit clients I ask them what they employ social media for and almost everyone has the same answer: "We're not sure really. Marketing mostly, I suppose." In other words, few companies I come across have any real plan for social media or any strategic thinking associated with it. Simply signing up for every social network, creating a profile, and then hoping this will lead to greater awareness of your business and what you sell is likely to lead to confusion for both customers and staff.

Imagine you run a bricks-and-mortar store where you simply have members of staff at some kind of central station. They do everything: they sell things to customers, deal with complaints and customer service issues, stock shelves, handle returns, package items for mail-order sales, and answer the phone. In fact, setting up a retail store like this would be a recipe for chaos. Instead, you would have a system in place that enabled staff to know whether they were working in customer service or sales. Equally, that system would provide clarity for customers, because they would know where to go to buy items or return them. Yet in the world of social media, many retailers are providing everything in every social network.

They do customer service and sales and staff communication all at the same time on Twitter, for example, which reduces clarity, and leads to unnecessary complexity.

Taking a strategic approach and using social networks for well-defined purposes can be simpler for customers and more manageable for staff. For instance, American airline JetBlue uses Twitter as a quick information service, a web page for customer service, and Facebook for promotions. The company provides customers with a clear idea of where to go to achieve specific aims, and when staff need to communicate something they also understand which method they need to employ.

BLUEPRINT

Although social media can benefit online stores in several ways, a strategic approach is required and the retailer has to decide on the precise purpose and aim of each social network it wants to use.

1. People want to chat about and share what they have bought from your store. Make sure you give them the opportunity to do this via social media add-ons.
2. Remember that using social media requires planning and monitoring in real time, meaning that you may require new staff and different working practices and processes.
3. Facebook allows people to engage with your brand, but that means you must engage with these people too.
4. Twitter provides the possibility for negative comments about your company to go viral unless you monitor the site and respond quickly.
5. Pinterest can be used to connect openly with potential customers who are in buying mode.
6. Google+ offers several potential benefits to retailers, especially in showing off expertise to information-seeking shoppers.

8

CAN THE RETAILER BE TRUSTED?

A major concern when shopping on the internet is that anyone can set up a shop online. Sometimes web shops can be fake, in fact positively fraudulent.

In 2009, several people were duped by one online shop that claimed it had the new Nintendo Wii Fit in stock. They only realized when the game system failed to arrive. By 2012, the issue of fake online shops had become such a problem that Lars Schmidt Larsen, CEO of Denmark's ecommerce foundation, had to issue a statement to consumers specifically warning them against three known bogus stores.

According to the UK Trading Standards Institute, fake luxury brand websites alone attract over 120 million global visits each year and lead to £82 billion being spent on counterfeit goods. Every year now a World Counterfeiting Day is held to bring the problem to public attention. As a result, consumers want to be certain that the shop they are considering buying from is a real one.

Eye-tracking studies demonstrate that people check things like a visible phone number on the top right of your site. If they can see that you are willing to take calls, you must be a real company, goes the reasoning. Also, some people scroll all the way down to the bottom of long pages and linger there for a short while. It appears they are looking for things like a physical address and a clickable email link, so that they know they can contact you.

Even so, many legitimate websites omit signals such as a physical presence and the willingness to be contacted: simple but important devices that will increase trust in your shop, particularly if they are on every page (top and bottom), not merely the front page or a contact page.

> If you are a registered business, it is a legal requirement in many nations to display your contact details on every website page.

Do other people trust the store?

If people do trust your site to be a real one from the physical signals you display, what they then want to know is whether other people trust you.

To see an analogy in the real world, take a holiday to the island of Lanzarote and go to Puerto del Carmen on the southeast coast. This is a popular holiday resort and along the seafront are dozens of restaurants. In the early evening, having showered and dressed after a day in the sun, holidaymakers are out in force, looking for somewhere to have a meal. You can watch them wander up and down, reading menus and then glancing inside the restaurant before moving on. What exactly are they looking for? They want to see whether there are other people inside. Few people want to be first and besides, if a restaurant is empty it implies that few people like its food. They want "social proof" that a particular establishment is worthwhile. Many people also have their mobile phone in their hand, checking a site like TripAdvisor to find additional evidence.

In the same way, people online like to see that they are not the first person to have bought a particular item – unless they're in a competitive race, such as wanting to be the first to get hold of the latest smartphone. Overall, people only buy things other people buy. In bricks-and-mortar stores we do this subconsciously by seeing what other people are doing. Social media can also help us decide what to buy, whether we do that online or offline. However, when people are in "buy now" mode online they don't want to go and ask their friends what they think. They need to see social proof right now that the item they are considering buying is worth paying for.

That is why star ratings and customer reviews are so important. They provide that third-party evidence that the product is worth buying. However, be careful how you display these reviews. An Australian study gave volunteers two sets of information about fictional coffee brands.[1] One was positively reviewed and the other negatively. However, after the volunteers had read the information they were told there had been a mistake, that the brand labeled negative was actually positive and vice versa. Another group of volunteers were given the information, but not told that a mistake had been made. The researchers, from the University of Melbourne, asked the participants to give ratings of the coffee companies. The people who had seen the positive information but were told that this was incorrect still rated the company highly. In other words, the original information lingered: what people hear or read first about a brand appears to influence their feelings about it, even in the light of subsequent information that suggests an alternative view.

For online retailers this means making sure that your most highly rated reviews remain at the top of the list. Some software for reviews on internet shops merely lists the reviews and ratings in chronological order. You are going to gain more sales if you don't do this, but instead list the ratings with the most positive at the top.

> TIP: Include instant star ratings and review systems on your website. This may help discourage people from going to central review sites where you have no control over the order of comments.

Ratings aren't all they're cracked up to be

One of the things any author wants is rave reviews for their book. So I really hope you will go along to Amazon, find the page for *Click.ology*, and give me your five-star review... Thank you. However, I am also aware that other books cover some of the material I have written about. A few of these other authors might not like the competition from me, so there is a chance they will go along to Amazon and say nasty things about this book, giving it zero stars or maybe just one or two. They hope that by doing so it will bring down the average star rating, putting sales of this book at risk.

The problem of fake reviews and ratings is a growing one online, particularly from unscrupulous companies that think they can gain commercial advantage by denigrating the competition. Companies such as Amazon do try to prevent fake accounts and consequently fictitious reviews being created. However, many online shops still suffer from sham reviews for products they are selling. User registration helps avoid this problem to some extent, but it needs to be a simple process, otherwise it is offputting to the real, honest reviewers you need.

There is also another growing problem: payment for reviews. Many big brands are paying bloggers and well-connected people on social networks to write positive reviews about them. According to analysts Gartner Inc., by 2014 up to 15% of reviews will have been paid for.

Even so, people like seeing reviews. Travel industry news site Tnooz claims that 95% of visitors to hotels claim reviews are untrustworthy; yet 53% of people say that they would not book a hotel without reviews. In spite of people not trusting reviews and being aware of the extent of potential fraud, they still want to see them. For the online retailer, this means accepting that some bad reviews and fake ratings will exist, but that this is better than having no ratings or reviews at all. Social proof operates at a sub-conscious level, so people will get a feeling for your overall level of reviews, rarely plumbing the depths for any details.

Trust is a gut instinct

In spite of all the complicated decision-making pathways that exist in our brain, which can be seen in operation when we are inside a brain scanner, we operate to a significant degree on "gut instinct." That's because the emotional centers of our brain tend to get infor-mation more quickly than the thinking areas. The emotional centers have communicated their findings to our subconscious before our conscious brain even gets the first inkling of a thought.

This was demonstrated in a clever experiment at Tel Aviv University by Professor Marius Usher.[2] He got people to look at a computer screen on which they were shown pairs of numbers very quickly and they had to calculate a sum from those numbers. However, the numbers were flashed so rapidly that they had no chance of actually doing the calculation: the only option was to guess. The more numbers they saw, the more accurate their guesses became. This study showed that people are very good at making an intuitive assessment when they are presented with a large amount of data.

That is why intuition or gut instinct is so powerful online. People are assessing a complex array of information when they look at your online shop. They want to know whether the shop is real, whether it has social proof, and whether they can find their way around. At the same time, they are seeking to find out whether it is "for them" based on the kind of shopper they are. And all this occurs before they actually process any written information. They are computing such an array of data that their intuition has to kick in, giving them a gut instinct about whether or not it is worth staying on this particular website.

For retailers this means one thing: if your website doesn't tick all the "gut reaction" boxes, people will click away within a fraction of a second. It means that trust in your website is dependent on more than merely signals of security – it relies on the complete picture. How can you design your site with this in mind?

You want your site to look good, of course, but focusing on aesthetics is not as important as focusing on the instinctive impression the design produces. For instance, if you are selling designer watches worth thousands of pounds, your website design and typography need to suggest this. However, if you are selling cheap watches for around £10 each on the same beautifully designed website, there will be a psychological mismatch for a potential customer, occurring from what is known as cognitive dissonance. Match the design to the expectations of the audience so that they instinctively know they are on the right site and can therefore trust it. If you have a 99p shop, your website must look like it sells 99p items, otherwise cognitive dissonance will make people think your business is "fishy" or up to something. The design of your website is a significant factor in conveying subconscious signals of trustworthiness.

BLUEPRINT

If people don't trust your online shop, no amount of clever marketing or sales patter will get them to buy from you. So you need to encourage trust among your customers and happily that is straightforward to achieve.

1. Put your address, phone number and email address on every page.
2. Ensure that you exhibit social proof on your site with reviews and ratings.
3. Accept that you will receive fake reviews, but try to weed them out.
4. List your reviews in order of positivity, with the best ones at the top.
5. Make sure that your website looks professional and is up to date and error free, as this will influence your visitors' gut instinct about you.
6. Ensure that your website is appropriate in appearance and design to what you sell.

9
AVOIDING THE CONS

One of my most treasured possessions is a gold Classic Century ballpoint from American quality pen manufacturer Cross. It has my initials engraved on the side, and I have had it since 1979. It was given to me by musician Bryan Ferry as a gift. At the time I worked as a press officer at Polydor Records, where I looked after the Roxy Music account, among others. During the year I had helped obtain publicity for the song "Angel Eyes," which had become the 49th top-selling single of the year. Even though I truly appreciated the pen and still treasure it today, I know the gift was in recognition of the significant amount of work I had done.

You very seldom receive a gift that is completely free, without strings attached or without it being in return for something else. Yet that's precisely what many online shops and websites would have people believe. They want customers to think that they are getting something for nothing, or that if they buy now they will get a massive array of free bonuses.

Many so-called internet marketing experts will tell you that you have to give away bonus products to help sell your main items. Steve Salerno, who exposed the world of the self-help industry in his book *SHAM*, pointed out that on one website an ebook called *Should You Stay or Should You Go?* was being sold with no fewer than seven bonus free items.[1] Offers like this are commonplace; indeed, as you trawl across the web, it seems as though there is some kind of competition between marketers to see just how many bonus products they can stuff into a sales page.

The theory is that people will think: "Wow, what great value! I only pay for one thing and get all this for nothing." It's a nice theory, but it's not true. Research on the psychology of choice suggests that bonus products can actually work against an online shop. In a study at Stony Brook University, New York, professor of marketing Michael Kamins found that freebies could contribute to products being devalued.[2] Adding bonus products based on "buy this and get all this free as well" doesn't actually make people feel as though they are gaining anything.

For example, let's say you sell a training course and offer free books that are worth, in your estimation, £150. If someone decides not to buy the training course but quite fancies the idea of the books, they will not be prepared to pay £150 for them because you have devalued them by giving them away for free. Bonus items cannot be sold separately for their intended price later on because the purchasers have already mentally devalued them – "If you were prepared to give them away free they can't be worth as much as you claimed."

This suggests that the popular "buy one, get one free" (BOGOF) campaigns so beloved of real-world supermarkets damage profitability in the long term. They are great for short-term cash flow, but when the promotion is over, consumers won't pay the individual prices again because they have mentally devalued the single product. This is also true online. If you sell a product but give away a bonus, you devalue that bonus for future sales. At the same time, the presence of the bonus devalues the brand and everything else you are trying to sell. Bonus items do appear to help clinch a sale in a wavering mind, so they can improve turnover, but you also need to focus on profitability and they are not so good for that.

The plethora of websites offering "free gifts" and bonuses probably believe that they are acting on the psychological principle of reciprocity – when someone does something positive for you and you feel indebted to them so want to do something good in return, you want to "return the favor." But reciprocity only operates between individuals: people do not reciprocate anonymously.

TIP: To avoid devaluing your brand, your products, and your online shop, don't go in for freebies. They may provide a short-term gain, but they will have negative impacts in the long term.

Sorry, you haven't won a prize

Frank Furness is a non-stop salesman: he is a tour-de-force of sell-ing. You can see him at sales and marketing events throughout the world, telling people how to sell and how to market things online. Frank sells dozens of products himself, such as DVDs and books, audio packages and software. At the end of every talk, people queue up to buy from him.

Frank told me that he has a favorite technique that helps him get more sales. In each of his talks he asks a question that means someone in the audience has to put their hand up. He will say that the first person to put up their hand in answer to his question will receive a prize – one of his books or DVDs. Of course, in a room full of several hundred people, he cannot really see who put their hand up first, so he chooses someone at the back of the room with their hand up. He then steps off the stage and hands the prize to someone in the *front* row, with the words: "Could you pass this to that lady at the back?" The book he is giving away then has to be passed between dozens of hands and is seen close up by scores of people. They all feel much closer to the item and are keener to buy it after the talk.

Few prizes have such a value, however, especially online. Many of the worst kinds of internet scams suggest that you have won a prize, and all you have to do is "click here" to get it, or enter your email address and it's yours – well done! The worst of these tricks install software on your computer to collect your private information, or to infect it with a virus and use it as part of a much wider hacking scheme. Obviously, such attempts to lure you into getting a prize are illegal. Yet in spite of this, you can find legitimate websites using the same kinds of schemes to try to get more people onto their mailing lists. Indeed, you can find websites telling you this is a good way of building your list. Don't believe them. The only mailing list worth having is one where people want to be on it because they like what you offer.

Furthermore, research suggests that giving rewards to peo-ple just doesn't work for the company doing the giving. A study at Case Western Reserve University in Cleveland, Ohio looked at the behavior of people after they had received a surprise win or loss during a game of chance. The researchers discovered that no matter whether the surprise was positive or negative, the individual's risk-taking behavior (in this case gambling) was reduced in the short term.[3] Clearly, this has implications for people trying to sell online, because buying is often a risk-taking behavior – people risk their money on the assumption that what they are buying is going to help them in some way. In other words, giving away prizes reduces your sales potential, at least in the short term.

> TIP: Only give away prizes if there is going to be a reasonable gap in time between the prize being handed out and the sales offer. Otherwise, prizes do not help sales.

No one really wants to help you

Similar to the "you have won a prize" fraud is the "we can help you" trick. A typical example of this is when you visit a web page and up pops a window saying, "Your computer is infected with a dangerous bug. Click here and we'll remove it for you." It sounds plausible and legitimate, but it is anything of the sort. The window that pops up may feature several official-looking signs, names, and apparent links and is designed to make you think it is reputable, but in fact it is a swindle to try to frighten you into buying a particular kind of software.

The psychological principle that the scammers think they are using is obedience to authority. Experiments conducted by American psychologist Stanley Milgram in the 1960s showed that when people are confronted with authority they tend to do what they are told, even if they would normally disagree with what they are being asked to do. In his experiments at Yale, Milgram set up an elaborate test that made volunteers think they were applying electric shocks to a fellow volunteer; 65% of them were seemingly happy to turn the electricity up to 450 volts. In fact the person receiving the "shocks" was an actor and no electricity was involved, but the research demonstrated that because the volunteers believed

Image courtesy of http://www.bleepingcomputer.com/virus-removal/ remove-fbi-anti-piracy-warning-ransomware

the person telling them to administer the shocks was in a position of authority, they did as they were told.[4]

This classic study is often used by unscrupulous marketers to suggest that if your website is an authority people will do as it tells them. The pop-up windows that suggest a person's computer is infected with a virus use this technique. Pop-ups are small windows that insert themselves above the main browser page and are often used for advertising, but this particular variety has a more sinister purpose. Such scam pop-ups try to look authoritative and official, thereby making people more susceptible to their messages. Some even suggest that they are from the FBI and contain the logos of antivirus software firms.[5] They claim that your computer is locked and that you have to pay a fine. The effect of this kind of scam is that the more unscrupulous companies try to use the psychology of obedience to authority, the more we doubt that such authority actually exists, because our growing experience is that it is all a fraud.

In 2008 things were different: people did not spot the fraudulent messages very well at all, according to research conducted at North Carolina State University.[6] However, by 2011 people had become increasingly annoyed and aware of pop-up messages, as revealed by a study from the Florida Institute of Technology.[7] Indeed, web browsers now have pop-up blocking software built in as standard. The result for ethical shop owners is that legitimate advertising pop-ups are less valuable than they once were because of the annoying activities of unscrupulous marketers.

> TIP: Avoid using pop-up windows on your website – overall they lower the respect people have for your business, thereby reducing your sales potential.

Squeezing only makes the pips squeak

One of the most popular uses of pop-ups online is the "squeeze" technique. A squeeze page is a web page that offers you no way out unless you either close the window or give the site your email address. There are no links anywhere, no home page button, and no navigation. All you can do is fill in the box to request more information. Once you do that, you are taken to the main website or some other page where you can download the freebie for which you have now signed up. The whole technique is designed to squeeze information out of you. Once you have entered your name into such a box you are usually inundated with emails suggesting that you buy all sorts of products, usually from affiliate links.

The theory behind such pages is that if you generate enough traffic to a squeeze page, and then send the hapless people who sign up hundreds of emails, eventually enough of them will buy your products for you to be able to make a good living. This may work for some, but for most people who try it the failure rate is very high.

Let's look at the numbers. The average conversion rate on the internet is 2%. That implies that only 2% of people who enter a squeeze page are likely to sign up. Once you start emailing them, an average of 2% are likely to click on a link in your email, and an average of 2% of those are likely to buy. So if you managed to get 2,500 people on your email list through your squeeze page, only 50 of them would click on a link, and only one of them would buy a product. However, to get the original 2,500 people signed up to the mailing list you would need 125,000 visitors to the original squeeze page – that's an awful lot of people for one sale.

Furthermore, some basic psychological research implies that squeeze pages are not a good idea in the first place. In a study of nursery school children in the 1970s, Yale professor Mark Lepper established the "overjustification effect." This occurs when people who get some kind of reward for an activity become demotivated about the activity itself because of the reward. In other words, if you fill in your email address on a squeeze page to get some kind of free report, you end up being less interested in the item you are being sent and the resulting page to which you are diverted. How many free offers have you signed up for, downloaded the ebook, and have yet to read the content? Squeeze pages *reduce* the engagement of your buyers, rather than increasing it.

> TIP: Avoid squeeze pages. You will maintain or enhance your reputation without them, plus you will avoid the potential reduction in engagement with your material.

You cannot make a million this afternoon

One of the biggest misconceptions on the internet is the notion that by setting up shop online you can become an almost instant millionaire. The web is littered with the broken dreams of those who were convinced they could make a million by teatime. The trick, by the way, is to have a simple ebook that tells your customers to set up a website telling people how to make millions, which sells a "secret," which is an ebook telling their customers how to set up a website to sell an ebook that has a "secret" – and so on and so on. The promise of millions only works for the first person in the chain, who sells millions of books to hapless individuals who think they can become rich without working for it.

But you knew this wasn't possible, didn't you? In fact, you didn't even have to think about it – you just "knew." There is plenty of psychological research confirming that our gut instinct is right far more often than it is wrong. If you feel in your heart that something isn't right, then it almost certainly isn't.

Research on gut instinct and financial matters was conducted in 2012 by researchers at the University of Exeter in the UK. This showed that even if we are likely to benefit financially from something we are being offered, we still sometimes defer to our heart rather than our head to make the ultimate decision.[8] So when you see a website offering you the opportunity to become an instant millionaire you may think you'd like the money – logically, who wouldn't? – but your heart tells you to forget it. If you are in any doubt at all about whether or not to buy something from a website, trust your gut. This means that if your business makes extravagant claims for its products or services, potential customers are likely to hold back because their gut instinct says it must be too good to be true.

> TIP: Avoid making claims that cannot be substantiated or sound too wild and extreme. People will not believe you and you devalue your business as a whole.

Envy is a negative emotion

Another trick many online marketers attempt is to show you that if you run your online shop the way they have run theirs, you will become just like them. They then proceed to show you pictures of their new Ferrari, their fantastic home beside the beach in some island idyll, together with their gorgeous partner sporting a Rolex watch. This is supposed to stimulate your desire to achieve a similar goal through envy. It doesn't work. Similarly, if your retail operation tries to show what customers can gain by buying your products, this can work against you.

One of the problems with creating envy is that it can raise stress hormones, which in turn affect thinking powers. As Dr. Art Markman, a psychologist from the University of Texas, said on the website Psychology Today:

> *When you are experiencing envy, it seems to get in the way of doing other thinking. There is quite a bit of research suggesting that stressful emotions can get in the way of thinking. Envy is like stress in that it is a negative emotion.*[9]

If you are trying to sell something, one of the worst things you can do is create negative emotions – what you want is to inspire positive emotions in your customers. As explained earlier, people conduct a great deal of assessment on what to buy with their "heart," by which we mean the emotional centers of the brain. So employ positive emotions such as humor on your website and in your advertising; negative emotions like envy can work against you.

> TIP: One of the most positive emotions is humor. Making your customers smile is likely to increase sales. Some of the most widely shared videos on YouTube are funny adverts.

The scams don't work

The vast number of online cons, swindles, and frauds all seem to think they are tapping into our brains in some way or another to make us more likely to buy what is on sale in their internet shop. However, either the psychological principles they are depending on have been bent beyond recognition, or they simply do not work in the way these scammers want them to.

Because there is a great deal of negative selling online, this creates a negative sales environment for even ethical, legitimate shops, which find it more difficult to sell as much as they would like because the scams and unethical behavior contribute to an overall increase in suspicion about online shopping.

BLUEPRINT

There are plenty of scam-style shops online, and these are affecting the sales of ethical stores because everyone is tarred with the same brush. In order to avoid being associated with negative selling practices, it is important to set up your online shop in a way that maximizes the impact of good sales practices.

1. Ignore any sales technique that your "heart" says is a bad idea.
2. Avoid the use of pop-ups.
3. Avoid offering freebies and items that are only delivered via squeeze pages.
4. Create web pages and marketing materials that trigger positive emotions only.

10

CREATING THE PERFECT ONLINE STORE

When American retailer Harry Gordon Selfridge opened his store on London's Oxford Street in 1909, he did something no other major retailer had done before. He allowed customers to touch the goods on sale, to experience what they were buying. Part of the radical change he brought about was to fill the entrance area with smells that would attract women into the store. Even today in Selfridges – and many other department stores across the world – you walk first into the perfumery department, which features a vast array of attractive smells to pleasure your nose. Harry Selfridge's device to get the recently emancipated women into his store has stood the test of time as being more than a trick.

But if you enter the store from its western side, via Orchard Street, you can't avoid the luscious smells of produce on sale in the Food Hall. Come in from the eastern end, through the doors in Duke Street, and either you'll face the instant delights of the champagne and caviar bar, or you'll be surrounded by displays of the latest women's fashion. Whichever door you use, it is instantly obvious what is on sale. Perhaps that is why in 2012 Selfridges won the title of "Best Department Store in the World."

Make it obvious what you're selling

People only give you a few seconds online: if you cannot demonstrate clearly and quickly what is on offer on your website, they leave because they don't want to waste their time.

You will undoubtedly have come across examples of online stores that are poorly designed and give no clue to what they're selling. I don't want to embarrass the website owners here by giving any examples, but each year the site Web Pages That Suck hands

out awards for the "World's Worst Websites." Site owners haven't
been taking much notice, it seems, because the awards are now in
their eighteenth year.

Luckily, there are plenty of other websites where it is completely obvious what is on sale from the moment you arrive. For
instance, German bike shop myownbike.de is completely clear
about what is on sale. You can't mistake it as selling anything else
other than bicycles.

Similarly, it is obvious what the New Zealand Wine Society
website is selling right from the moment it loads, and you are able
to click on an image of a wine bottle and buy a case directly from
the front page.

Sites like these work very well for utilitarian shoppers – as
explained in Chapter 3, people who know what they want and
want to get it now – because they show instantly that the shopper
is in the right place for their needs. Other sites will appeal to informational shoppers by making it clear from the start that they are
information based. Coarse fishing site gofishing.co.uk does this well.
There are obvious links to the company's shop if you do want to

buy, but the front page is clearly informational, with links to several in-depth articles about fishing as well as pages of tips and hints. This will appeal to the shopper who wants to do research first and buy second.

As another example, the Juicemaster store in Australia focuses on information delivery for the research-style shopper, while also making it obvious where to buy things if you've done enough research and want to go ahead and make a purchase.

Crucial to this instant recognition is deciding what kind of shopper a site is designed for. Are you aiming at the "buy now" kind of shopper or the information-seeking researcher? Of course, that doesn't prevent you from having two different websites, each angled to one of these styles of online shopping.

> TIP: Make it obvious what you sell, but also make it obvious what kind of website you are running – a "buy it now" shop or an "information" site.

Make the shopping process simple

In addition, your store needs to be straightforward and easy to buy from – it needs to be convenient. This means that the whole process, from selecting an item and adding it to the shopping cart to paying and checking out, must be smooth and able to be accomplished without difficulty. As we saw in Chapter 5, shopping cart abandonment occurs very frequently, and much of this is due to complexity in the process itself. The perfect online store has a shopping cart that works quickly and efficiently.

Unfortunately, the simplest way of enabling online shopping – with a single click – is not available as Amazon has patented it, although as already explained, the company only achieves one click because its shoppers have previously set up an account in which their credit card details are stored. In order to benefit from your best possibility of two clicks, your shopping cart will either need to have an account system in place or to present all the required fields, including credit card details, on one checkout page. Some shopping cart programs achieve this, but others do not; there's information on how to choose a shopping cart system later in the chapter.

> TIP: Minimize the number of clicks from product selection to final payment. The fewer the clicks, the better.

The perfect shopping cart also ensures that customers can go from cart to product details and back again. As outlined in Chapter 5, people often put things in their online basket and then want to go back to check some details before they pay. If the shopping cart loses their item, or they aren't able to return to the product details page (or anywhere else on the website), then they're likely to give up. So you need a seamless connection between the descriptive web pages and the back-office shopping cart system, so that customers can do what they like without losing items or losing their way.

One particular area where consumers have difficulty is the forms they have to fill in to enter their personal details, credit card information, and so on. Research shows that people become easily confused if these forms are arranged in two columns. Instead, design a single-column form, so that all the information can be entered in a linear process, which reduces the complexity.

A number of studies have revealed that "Buy Now" buttons can be offputting. Instead, a phrase on the button like "Proceed to Checkout" can often work better. Such subtle changes are often dependent on your market and demographic, therefore the perfect shop always "split tests" every element of its shopping system to ensure that customers can use it easily, as discussed in Chapter 5. For instance, one page might have a "Buy Now" button, the other a button that says "Order Now." Alternate visitors to the page are presented with one version or the other. Using web analytics software, it is then simple to see which page led to more items being bought, thereby telling you which wording is the more appealing to customers.

> It is not possible to give hard-and-fast rules about how to design shopping pages or shopping processes. Every group of customers is different, so the only way to achieve a perfect store is through continual testing.

One way of simplifying the shopping process is to have a comprehensive search facility on your site. Recently I was talking through with a potential client their issues with their online store and how they thought I might be able to help them. What they wanted to find out was why so many people typed something into the search box but then didn't click on any of the results. So I tested their search system, typing in a few words appropriate to the products they were selling. The results of my search told me everything I needed to know. The search facility only searched for products; it did not look for information anywhere else on the website. Customers can already see the products in the relevant area of the online store, so they are often looking for more than that when they search.

A perfect online shop has thorough and excellent search facilities. What is more, these should be in the place where most people look for them, in the middle or, failing that, toward the top right of the page. Google's search box is in the middle, so are Amazon's, eBay's, and Facebook's. That means that most people are familiar with a central search box, so the perfect shop will place it there – and it will work quickly and completely.

Another aspect of simplicity is a returns policy and facility, as discussed in Chapter 6. People tend to shop more often on a site where the returns process is clearly displayed, because they like to know they can send something back if it isn't suitable. If your store doesn't show how to return unwanted items, or makes it difficult for people to find this information, visitors are less likely to want to shop with you. So the perfect store has an easy-to-use returns system that is clearly visible.

One final aspect of the perfect shop is displaying a phone number, for reasons discussed in Chapter 8. While this isn't important for giant stores like Amazon that have tightly integrated and semi-automated customer service facilities, for most online stores customers like to know they can phone you should they have any questions. Indeed, some people may like to browse your store and then order by phone. The perfect online store will therefore feature a phone number where people most frequently look for it, at the top of the page – and it will be in a large, clear font.

Make sure people can see clearly how to pay

My local branch of retailer Marks & Spencer was one of the first in the UK to have a significant refit a few years ago. We had waited patiently while all the work was going on, and when the store reopened in its new guise I was keen to examine the changes. Some of them were excellent, including better displays and a more efficient pathway around the store, but as I shopped I realized I couldn't see anywhere to pay for my items. No matter where I looked, there were no "Pay Here" signs. So I did what most people would and that is walk toward the exit, where shops usually place the tills. However, in fact the new checkouts had been located in the middle of the store – not the obvious place to look, and a task made more difficult by a lack of signage and several clothing displays that were effectively hiding them.

It is frustrating when you cannot find where to give a company your money. As retail expert Paco Underhill points out, "the biggest single quandary in cash/wrap is where to put it."[1] Underhill cautions against locating the cash desk near the entrance, because doing so can lead people to leave the store or not fully explore it; nevertheless, that is where most retailers put it. If most stores have checkouts in the same position it is a case of familiarity breeding usability, not contempt. It means that people don't have to learn different principles of shopping for every store.

Online, the problem is that cash desks, shopping carts, and payment options are all over the place. And because people don't spend the time looking for them, as they would in a real-world store, they just leave the site and go to an online shop that is easier to use.

So where should the perfect online store have its checkout button or other "pay here" signage? Most people look for an online checkout on the top right of the page, because that is where it is located on Amazon and eBay, the sites where most online shoppers do most of their buying.

Don't worry about your website looking the same as any other online store. Your web designers might say things like "other sites put it there; you want to be different to stand out." In this respect, difference means invisibility. Shift your checkout away from the top right and it's like asking someone to drive a car that doesn't have pedals or a steering wheel. They could work out how to do it if they could be bothered, but it would be so much easier if the process was the one they're familiar with.

Use the colors that work best

Given that people land on your shop pages and disappear within fractions of a second if they're not interested, one of the few psychological weapons you have to attract attention and make shoppers linger is color. The colors on a web page are instantly recognized by the human eye, even if the visitor hasn't consciously realized they're looking at blue, red, or green. What is more, color interpretation is not only done by the visual center of the brain, but by areas that

detect motion and texture, for instance. Because various parts of
the brain are in use, even people who have a condition known as
achromatopsia, which means that they can't see color, are able to
interpret the color *differences*.

Colors are the most quickly recognized aspect of any web
page and much has been written about "color psychology," advis-
ing you on what colors mean and how to apply them to your
online store. Sadly, much of this "advice" is based on assumption
and hearsay rather than actual evidence. For instance, consider
what you might think about the color green. In Europe, people tend to link green with nature and recycling, but in South
America it is connected with death. Similarly, blue is associated
with patriotism in the US, but with healing in China. Color
is such a subjective issue that getting it right for your website
depends on the culture and the specific circumstances in which
your website will be viewed.

There has been very little research on the impact of color
online, particularly in relation to retail, and the studies that have
been done are inconsistent and confusing. In some tests of shopping
cart buttons red has been shown to lead to more clicks than green,
in a similar fashion to the color of prices discussed in Chapter 4,
but other studies claim that red doesn't work well; some claim that
blue helps sales while others perceived no differences. And color
does not always produce what you might think is the "common-
sense" reaction. For example, if you were studying ambient light
colors in an area where people were tasting wine, you might think
that drinking red wine under red lights might make drinkers more
connected to the wine and thereby that they would consider it
more positively. However, in one experiment the red light had no
effect on perceived taste, although when the wine was drunk under
blue lighting, people did report that the taste was bitterer.[2]

More than this, the colors people see depend on the kind of
monitor or screen they are using, the settings of their web browser,
whether their screen has natural light shining on it from a window,
and how the room lighting has been set up. You might design your
website with a bright red background, but what the visitor actually
sees could be orange because of these other influencing factors.

Nevertheless, for many retailers such as fashion stores, the colors are vital – if a customer wants to buy a red top, they won't consider one that looks pink, even if in reality it is red. To help ensure that visitors see the colors of its products in the best way possible, the website of online fashion retailer Asos is primarily black and white – almost the only colors you see are those of the items for sale. Furthermore, those items are photographed against a white or neutral background so that no color distractions or distortions occur.

This whole arena is so full of conflicting advice that there is only one solution – test, test, and test again, to see which colors and strategies work in your specific circumstances for your particular market.

Choose the most appropriate shopping cart

Type the phrase "best shopping cart" into Google and you end up with almost half a million results. If you go to the various review sites or directory listings, you discover two things: most of the review sites are not true reviews, since they are affiliate programs under which people are aiming to make money by persuading you toward a specific product; and secondly, the directories have widely varying listings. Indeed, one Top 10 listing of shopping carts presents an entirely different list to another so-called Top 10 directory. Confusing, isn't it?

The most important aspect of choosing a shopping cart program is to make sure it is completely flexible, allowing you to do exactly what is right for your marketplace. To help you decide on the right ecommerce system for your business, including the most suitable method of taking payments, there are ten questions you need to answer.

1. Do you need a merchant account?

A merchant account is a special kind of bank account that requires verification of you and your organization, using high levels of security. A merchant account is not necessary to conduct business online and take money. However, you will probably need one if you want to:

◆ Take orders by phone or fax.
◆ Take orders in person, such as in a bricks-and-mortar store.
◆ Receive the money quickly.
◆ Reduce your monthly fees and commissions.
◆ Sell certain products or services (such as "adult" items).
◆ Run any sizable retail operation.

2. What type of merchant account do you need?

There are two types of merchant account: one where you own the account and have a direct relationship with the bank issuing it; and a third-party account, where another company rents you space on its merchant account. PayPal, for instance, includes third-party merchant accounts as part of its business offering Website Payments Pro.

The difference between merchant accounts largely concerns pricing. Third-party merchant accounts are usually free to set up and can be started quickly, sometimes immediately after signing up. However, they attract much higher commission and monthly ongoing fees; some companies also keep your money for 30 days before you can access it. A standard merchant account features lower monthly fees and low commission rates on each transaction. It also gives you access to incoming funds within three days. However, there tends to be a start-up fee and the account takes longer to set up because of the security checks needed on you and your business. The standard merchant account provides you with greater flexibility, nevertheless.

3. Do you need a payment processor?

A payment processor is a service that takes credit card information from your customers and extracts the money from their account to pay it into your merchant account. Some companies that provide merchant accounts, such as RBS WorldPay, include a payment processor within their service. Other organizations, such as SagePay, are only payment processors and so you need a separate merchant account from a second supplier. PayPal Business is a complete package of payment processor and merchant account wrapped into one.

If you already have a merchant account for an existing offline business, such as a retail store, you will need an online payment processor. However, if you only operate online you can use a combination service – you do not need a separate merchant account and payment processor, unless you want to have different options in the future. For instance, if you have a merchant account and payment processor combined you stand a risk – albeit a small one – of not being able to take money from customers if the service breaks down or ceases operation. If you separate the services you would be able to reestablish your online payment facility more quickly.

For most niche stores, the decision comes down to PayPal or another package provider such as RBS WorldPay or SagePay. Remember that PayPal is the most widely recognized online payment system worldwide, with over 100 million active users, so the name recognition alone may be of benefit. Going the separate systems route with your own merchant account and a payment processor is more cumbersome and technically difficult, although this is often the preferred method for larger businesses because it is perceived to be more secure.

4. Do you need a virtual terminal?

If you want to take money on the phone, by fax, or from people who email you their details, rather than using a web page or shopping cart, and you do not have a full, standard merchant account, you will need a virtual terminal. This is a secure web page that you log into and then enter your customer's credit card details by hand. Some payment processor companies, such as SagePay, provide a virtual terminal as standard. RBS WorldPay charges a one-off set-up fee for this service. PayPal includes it within Website Payments Pro or as a stand-alone function.

5. Can you use an alternative to the merchant route?

It is possible to sell products and services online without having a merchant account or a payment processor. Many hosting companies offer complete ecommerce packages such as web shops and there are also specialist firms that provide online "shops in a box." In both these instances, once you've set up an account, usually for a monthly fee, you can sell your products and services using the system's own payment processing and merchant account.

The advantages of this route include the ability to be up and running within minutes. All you need to do is sign up, use a preformatted template, add your products, and away you go. However, there are limitations. You are restricted to the shop designs and layouts on offer, meaning that you may not be building the perfect store for your particular customers. Many of these services include hundreds of possible layouts and the ability to incorporate your own graphics and logos, but they are not as flexible as developing your own website. In addition, those that also offer payment processing tend to charge relatively high rates of commission and keep any income for a long period before you can extract it into your bank account.

6. Do you want to take subscriptions?

If you want to charge monthly subscriptions or you have some kind of membership site where you charge regular fees, take special care over the merchant account or payment processor you choose. Some don't offer this feature and others charge extra. For instance, RBS WorldPay Gateway Plus requires a one-off set-up fee in order to collect regular payments.

Be sure as well that any shopping cart software you use can also handle subscriptions or regular payments. Some can, but only with certain payment processors and not others. The lesson is, if you want to take subscriptions you need to check what is available very carefully indeed.

7. Do you need a shopping cart at all?

If you sell several products and people will potentially be buying more than one item, then a shopping cart is convenient. However, if you are only selling a single product, or people only buy one product or service at a time from you, a shopping cart can be an unnecessary diversion. Simply adding a "Buy Now" button and connecting that to PayPal may be all you require.

Even so, shopping carts do have attractions. First, many of them connect with online payment processors automatically. If you use PayPal buttons or a similar service, you have to code the buttons each time. With a shopping cart you usually only set up the connection once, and then each time you add a product or service the software automates the process for you. Furthermore, customers are comfortable with shopping carts because they are everywhere on the web. Having a shopping cart service on your website, over and above a simple "buy now" button, can improve customer confidence.

8. What kind of shopping cart do you need?

There are three main kinds of shopping cart:

◆ A *hosted* shopping cart, such as 1ShoppingCart or DPD, is where the service is on the company's servers and you rent usage of it. Usually you are allowed a limit in terms of the number of customers or the number of products and transactions you can have.
◆ A *stand-alone* shopping cart is software that can be downloaded and installed on your system, such as ShopFactory or Coffee Cup Shopping Cart Creator.

◆ A *scripted* shopping cart is a system that you need to install on your own web server. Such services include VirtueMart or ClickCartPro.

A hosted service is best if you are not very technical; the scripted services are the ones that require technical knowledge. Hosted services are usually less flexible because they have to cater for the majority of their users. If you want something that few other users also want, then a hosted service may not provide it, making it more difficult for you to produce a perfect store.

9. Do you sell downloads?

If you sell ebooks, software, music, video, or other digital goods your shopping cart or payment processor needs to be able to handle that kind of product. Many don't have this capability. Equally, many do not provide time-limited download links or other security measures that help prevent your digital goods from being shared or stolen. PayPal, for instance, allows the selling of downloads, but you need to add security software yourself, such as DLGuard. Usually, if you want to handle digital goods effectively, you need a scripted shopping cart system.

10. Are you technically minded?

Arranging to take money online requires technical skills. Either you have to set up a scripted retail system including some elements of coding, or you need to be able to connect several different services together, such as a merchant account, a payment processor, and a shopping cart. If you are not technically gifted, the amount of time you need to spend could be counterproductive; even hosted package systems, such as 1ShoppingCart, require some technical knowledge. For large retailers, of course, IT departments will manage all this. However, writing bespoke software and creating the perfect shopping cart system can be extremely costly and time consuming.

Clearly, choosing the right shopping system for the perfect online store isn't easy; it is much more complex than most businesses I have worked with have ever imagined. The issues you need to consider will be dealt with effectively if you answer the ten questions above. If you don't handle these issues carefully, the chances are that you won't have the right shopping software to enable you to produce exactly the right kind of shop for your particular shoppers.

Create customer engagement

Assuming that you do have a great shopping cart system that allows you maximum flexibility to match your customers' needs, the next element of the perfect store to consider is how your customers can engage with your online shop. As we saw in Chapter 7, people are keen to share their purchases with their friends. That means your site needs to have capabilities that allow people to share what they have bought on social networks such as Facebook, Twitter, Pinterest, and Google+.

Make sure that you include the option to tweet about purchases after someone has bought an item, for example on your order confirmation page. Equally, it is a good idea to include social sharing links in email receipts and order confirmations, offering people a further chance to be social about their purchases.

The other side of engagement is people giving you their views about your products and services. Mostly these are going to be positive, so you should encourage them. For instance, in 2012 retro T-shirt store TruffleShuffle encouraged its visitors to add reviews by offering a voucher for doing so.

While vouchers, money-off coupons, or gifts can all encourage reviewers to add their comments to your website, you have to make this easy for them. Some sites require separate registration and log-in before a customer can write a review. Why would they bother when all they want to say is a line or two about how much they like what they've bought? You reduce confusion and

make it more likely you will get reviews and ratings if you have a single-page, one-column form that is easily accessible. Remember, if people cannot easily review your products and services on your own site, they may well go to an external review site where they only need a single sign-on to review items from a wide range of suppliers and manufacturers.

Consider the example of the Baker's Oven, a bread maker sold by Breville in Australia. This has been reviewed considerably more times on Product Review Australia than it has on Breville's own site. To provide a review on the Breville site a customer has to click on "Add Your Review," which takes them to a point where they are told they need to log in. Clicking on that leads them to an account log-in page where, if they do not already have an account, they have to create one. By that time their motivation for offering a review has probably reduced considerably. In contrast, at Product Review Australia they can write a review, create an account, or log in from a single page that can be reached with one click.

A perfect online store will therefore have an easy-to-use product review system, as well as recognizable and simple methods of sharing purchases on social networks.

Demonstrate that you are security conscious

Security is a key concern for online shoppers. As detailed in Chapter 8, people are wary of stores that they do not know much about. Large, well-known sites can create a degree of trust through their brand image combined with significant amounts of experience. But many purchases are made on smaller websites or as one-offs, where the customer has no perception of the brand or company, nor any experience to go by. Therefore, in these circumstances an online store must display signals of trust to indicate that it is responsible.

As already discussed, simple things help, such as having a physical address, telephone number, and clickable email link at the bottom of every page. These indicate that you exist in the real world and are willing to be contacted. Also, put the logos of any trade or professional bodies you belong to in your page footer to demonstrate your credentials – and make sure that such logos are connected to your profile pages at those organizations, so that your visitors can click on them and check your company details. The logos of payment processors or credit cards that you accept can be linked to relevant pages on banking information sites to give further credibility to your store.

However, what is most important in online shopping security is the "https" protocol. This uses a process known as the Secure Sockets Layer, which encrypts credit card and personal information as it is transmitted on the internet. Web shoppers are aware that this system provides the visual reassurance of a locked padlock symbol in their browser. Indeed, if you have a merchant account or payment processor, you will be required to have a secure site as part of your agreement. With SSL you get a security certificate from an organization such as GeoTrust, Thawte, or Verisign, together with a logo that confirms your store is secure.

Furthermore, it is a good idea to have a security page on your website that confirms what you do to protect shoppers. One of the ways credit card data is stolen is for it to be physically removed from the premises of online shops, rather than through account hacking. For instance, unethical staff could log in to their internal system, print out customer credit card details, and then walk out of the office with the information in their pocket. A perfect online store will have a page that not only talks about the web security measures in place, but also provides reassurance on the physical security measures that you employ at your premises. People take it as read that large companies will have physical security, but for smaller companies what you do is worth emphasizing. That way you further reassure your customers, again increasing the likelihood of purchase.

BLUEPRINT

The perfect online store can be created by following these seven steps:

1. Make it obvious what you are selling with the right pictures and words that communicate in an instant what your shop is offering.
2. Simplify the product selection process, making it as smooth and easy as possible with a comprehensive search facility.
3. Show people where to buy and how to pay and make these elements of your site obvious.
4. Test the site design and colors – what works in one market might not work as well in another.
5. Use the shopping cart and payment processes that include the right features for your market.
6. Incorporate social engagement tools, such as comment and review facilities, as well as the opportunity for people to share their purchases easily on social networks.
7. Demonstrate that you are security conscious and that you take care of customer information.

11

THE FUTURE OF ONLINE SHOPPING

There is no doubt that online shopping is a phenomenon that is here to stay. In 2012, the number of goods sold online worldwide went up by 18% compared with the previous 12 months – and that had been a record year. Even in China, where most of the population does not have access to the internet, online shopping is a multibillion industry. At any moment, tens of thousands of people are busy shopping on the web, and some companies are taking mind-boggling amounts of money. According to Amazon's 2012 annual report, its net product sales for the year were almost $52 billion, equivalent to $1,640 every second – that's popular. Meanwhile, around $4,600 goes through eBay's tills every second, and the company expects the $145 billion it currently transacts each year to go up to $300 billion by 2015, more than the GDP of most countries.

Nevertheless, even in the UK, the world's leading nation for online shopping with an average annual spend of £1,083 per head, 90% of all shopping is still done in bricks-and-mortar stores. And many businesses are confused and unsure, as they are discovering that what works offline does not necessarily lead to success online, and vice versa.

There is a generational influence here. Older people are less familiar with online shopping, so when they want to buy something their first thought is to go to a real-world shop. However, this is changing too. I was recently talking with the chief executive of a major fashion chain that has hundreds of physical stores as well as an online presence. Its internet shop has not been as successful as the company would like, which it put down to the average age of its shoppers, who tend to be in their 60s. Yet since the growth in popularity of the iPad and other tablet devices, the online store has seen massive growth. Tablet devices are very easy to use and older people find them less technical, so as a result seniors are increasingly shopping online.

The current trend in mobile take-up not only means increased sales through your business's online channel, it also means changes in the demographics of your website visitors. Not only are the characteristics of shoppers altering, the number of customers is also growing and their requirements are shifting too. Never before have retailers been in a situation where so many different changes are happening at the same time, and at such ferocious speed.

Daryl Conner points out in his book *Managing at the Speed of Change* that we have two options when it comes to rapid change: we can become negative and concerned about the situation, or we can see the change as an opportunity.[1] In many companies, the former option takes hold. Doom and gloom set in as people worry about the amount of work required to adapt their business to the current changes, let alone deal with the new ones around the corner. This is reflected in several studies. For instance, in Australia a higher percentage of people shop via their mobile than in any other country, perhaps not surprising considering the distances involved. Yet as media website mUmBRELLA reported at the beginning of 2013, only 36% of online stores in Australia have mobile-friendly websites. This is a symptom of the degree to which change is overwhelming many businesses, leading them to delay rather than act.

In 2012 I was contacted by a large bricks-and-mortar retailer that specialized in selling products to businesses. It had an online store of a kind, but still mostly relied on sales reps visiting target customers with a catalog in hand, hoping to take orders. The directors of the company accepted that this was rather quaint and old-fashioned and that their customers were demanding a full-service online shop, so they came to me to help them with the strategy they needed to adopt. I had several meetings with the chief executive and the relevant board director, and I spoke to a number of staff members about their ideas. I even had conversations with their customers. Nevertheless, a year later my proposals have not yet been put into effect.

I asked the chief executive why the company still did not have a full online store. He told me that the necessary changes would mean that some of his sales representatives would no longer be required, while new staff would need to be appointed to take on technical roles. The company would also have to change the way it promoted the products on sale as well as how it analyzed its activities. These were, of course, all points I had discussed with him and raised in my report. In effect, the change required was simply too big.

Online music sales should have been pioneered by the music industry itself, but music companies were focused on trying to ban people from listening to music digitally. Instead, the online music business was invented by a niche computer company that, at the time, was selling Macintosh desktops and laptops, largely to the creative sector. Similarly, the search engine was invented by a couple of students doing their PhDs, not by Yellow Pages or Kelly's; the first online bookshop was the idea of a computer network specialist from Wall Street. Why did the people who previously "owned" an industry or sector relinquish control to someone who was effectively an interloper? It was largely down to their unwillingness to accept change.

Businesses who want to thrive in this fast-moving retail environment need to be open to change and to learning from both online and offline experiences. If they fail to do this, they risk being outflanked by more flexible competitors – or quite simply going out of business.

Change is not always different

I first met public relations expert Nigel Morgan almost 10 years ago at a business event in Newbury, in the south of England. I was giving a presentation about blogging, then a comparatively new online technology. At the beginning of the meeting I asked how many people were actively involved in blogging and Nigel was the only person in the room to raise his hand. I then said that blogging would be essential to the success of small local firms. Indeed, I forecasted that if the businesses in that room were not blogging within 12 months, they would not be in business in year five. Nowadays, Nigel tells this story himself, adding two interesting facts. First, he was the only person at the event who carried on blogging; in fact he did even more of it. Secondly, the other businesses that were at the meeting are no longer trading.

I'm not telling you this to impress you with my powers of prediction, but rather to point out that these businesses thought blogging was new and different, some quirky thing that only geeks did. They were therefore mildly concerned about the technology and viewed it as something that could be set aside until another day when there was "spare time," whatever that is. The result was that they ignored it.

In fact blogging is merely another form of "content marketing." This phrase is popular online today, although politicians and religions have done this for centuries, spreading their word in leaflets, posters, and newsprint, and businesses themselves have always produced marketing publications.

This kind of problem persists in several other areas of online shopping. For instance, website analytics sounds grand, complex, and technical; indeed, technically it is quite complicated. However, the concept of analyzing how people use your shop, what they are interested in, how long they spend doing certain things, and what are the most popular items is nothing new – it's been standard fare for retailers for decades. Yet I meet online businesses who are concerned about analytics because they perceive it as new and different, meaning that they fail to undertake it and consequently miss out on potentially important information that might boost their success.

When I ask businesses what they measure on their websites, the most common answer is "hits." If you are only considering hits you are merely measuring how many times each element of your web page has been loaded, which is comparable to a real-world business counting the number of people walking through the door. Just because a visitor has loaded a web page does not necessarily mean that they have engaged with it in any meaningful way.

The attitude that new implies complex and that it will lead to more problems is a considerable barrier to many businesses grasping the real benefits of online retail. Far from the psychology of internet shoppers being an obstacle, it is the psychology of the retailers themselves that is the problem.

We have the technology

As an example of this intransigence, consider my recent trip to a bookshop in my home town. I wanted to get a book on small business marketing, but I had no specific title in mind, so my first problem was to find the relevant section. I went to the general business books area, but it was impossible to find the ones on marketing because all the books were stocked alphabetically according to the author's surname. That's fantastic if you know the name of the author you're looking for, but otherwise finding the right book is time consuming and frustrating. A book on leadership might be next to one on sales, which is next to another on accounting. Online, I'm used to finding a book in seconds by typing the subject in the search box of an online bookstore. I can click on the book, look inside it, and order it quickly; if it's in ebook format, I can be reading it in less than a minute. Back in my local bookstore, it takes more than a minute to find the relevant shelves, let alone track down an individual book.

But here's the rub: the technology exists – indeed, has existed for many years – to allow physical bookshops to offer instant search facilities so that you can go in, tap on a screen, and be shown exactly where your book is in the shop. Bookshops don't offer this service because they haven't acknowledged that people's demands have changed. They are letting online shops with efficient search possibilities take their customers from under their noses.

Of course, technology transfer isn't all one way. Take touch, an essential part of selling products for any clothes retailer. Go into a bricks-and-mortar store and you see people touching clothing all the time. Often they're not even aware they're doing this, because retailers usually pack the rails close together, forcing people to feel the fabrics as they brush past.

Clothing retailers sell plenty of fashion on the web, but when people order clothing online their first chance to touch it only comes when it arrives at their home, and often they don't like what they feel. A study by Bank Credit Suisse discovered that around half of all clothing ordered during the run-up to Christmas is returned in January.[2] While this could also be related to sizing or the vagaries of gift purchasing, closer cooperation with internet technologists might help alleviate the problem.

It has been possible to transmit the sense of touch across the internet for more than a decade and some whacky projects demonstrate its potential.[3] For instance, Professor Adrian Cheok, from Keio University in Tokyo, was the first person to hug a chicken virtually. At one end, a live chicken wore a tiny jacket that was connected to the internet. At the other end, Professor Cheok held a toy-like replica chicken that was also linked to the system. He was able to feel the real chicken moving, even though he was not actually holding the live bird. This example might seem silly, but using this kind of haptic technology you can shake hands with someone on the other side of the planet and feel their response.

Other seemingly out-of-reach features are now possible, such as robotic sales assistants and virtual fitting rooms.

CASE STUDY: FITS.ME

Technology company Fits.me believes that it offers a solution to avoiding the high number of returns in online clothing sales with its innovative "virtual fitting room." This allows customers to enter their measurements on a clothing site and then select a garment to see how it would look on them. For instance, they could see how a particular size of item looked on them, whether it was tight or generous. After all, what one manufacturer calls medium may be equivalent to small from another.

According to Fits.me, its system has enabled online clothing retailers to reduce their item return rate by a massive 77%.

Importantly, fashion retailers who use this virtual fitting room have also increased their online sales conversion rate by 57%.

Fits.me uses robotized mannequins, which go through a whole range of shapes and body sizes, resulting in each garment being photographed thousands of times. That means there is always an image that can be shown on the website that matches an individual person's body size and shape. It's like having a fitting room mirror in front of you, only online.

And that is not all. When I first wrote about the internet in 1994, I commented on the potential for the "Internet fridge." People thought I was daft, but I'd seen some early prototypes of a refrigerator with a computer monitor in the door. The idea was that you could connect to the internet while doing your cooking and order any missing ingredients from an online shop. Now you can buy that fridge from manufacturers such as Samsung. You can leave messages on the front, you can save and retrieve recipes, and you can shop; you can even listen to music while you cook. It won't be long before such fridges can automatically check the use-by dates on your food, send you a note saying "do not eat this," and automatically order a replacement from your favorite online supermarket.

The "internet of things" is now well and truly with us. Korean electronics company LG makes internet-connected washing machines and dishwashers, and you can even get cushions for your sofa that can monitor when your pet jumps up on your precious furniture, alerting you wherever you may be in the world and allowing you to send some kind of noise or stimulation to get the animal to jump down.

The presence of such seemingly science fiction items prompts a question for many online retailers: What new technologies are they using to improve their offering? All that is holding internet shopping back is a lack of creative thinking. Existing businesses that fail to adapt could soon be outmaneuvered by opportunistic players from outside the retail sector that create start-ups combining technologies and giving them first-mover advantage.

Niche sites will offer choice and convenience

Many bricks-and-mortar retailers are wasting time trying to recreate their offline stores online, instead of doing something that matches their customers' needs and expectations. Some of them are yet to take up the online challenge at all. In the meantime, the online space is dominated by big players such as Amazon and eBay, with Google also muscling into retail with its app distribution platform Google Play, among other initiatives.

At the other end of the scale are many niche players focusing on specific products for particular markets and groups of customers. For instance, if you suddenly decide you need a fake mustache, there is a niche site just for that: facetache.com. In the past, you were only likely to get a fake mustache from a party store or a toyshop. It was probably not the most popular line, so the shop would maybe only stock the three most profitable varieties. Yet at facetache.com 60 different fake mustaches are available. Niche online stores like this can provide variety and choice that would not otherwise be possible and are one reason online shopping is so successful.

The little secret behind facetache.com, however, is that the owner of the store, Australian web designer Andrew Dyster, doesn't stock any fake mustaches at all. Nor does he buy them and ship them to you. Instead, all the items in his store are "affiliate links" to a variety of different suppliers. He saves you the bother of having to search the web for the specific fake mustache you might desire by aggregating a selection from various suppliers into one convenient, niche store. This is another reason online shopping is so popular – convenience. In fact, this is such an important way of providing niche shopping that specialist software such as PopShops and Datafeedr allows retailers to choose from a variety of different product lines and suppliers in order to populate a shop with niche products automatically. This means that small retailers can establish shops online that would not be possible to create offline; there would simply not be the footfall in one town in one country for a bricks-and-mortar shop selling fake mustaches.

Customer service will improve

Since anyone can set up a niche shop for just a few pounds, customers are becoming more discerning. If the online shop does not operate well, they can click away and find an alternative. As a result, the successful online shops are the ones that focus on customer service.

Nevertheless, customer service is inadequate at many internet retailers. In many instances that is because the store owners are home-based individuals employing affiliate marketing techniques to earn some extra cash. To them it is not a real business, but something that might provide them with enough money for a holiday each year. Unfortunately, there is no easy way of customers distinguishing between a site like this and a proper business. Hence, shoppers are gravitating toward the better-known online stores, as long as they provide an excellent level of customer service.

I recently bought an item from a large online store. Unfortunately, when I received the item the price on the invoice was double what I'd been expecting to pay. I checked the website and sure enough, I was right about the price quoted. So I logged into the customer service pages and chose the relevant complaint area. The site gave me three options for proceeding with the issue, but recommended I used the online chat facility. I took up the offer and within 30 seconds the staff member had apologized and refunded my credit card with the relevant amount. Within another 30 seconds or so, I had received an email from the person I had chatted with, confirming our conversation and the refund.

A similar situation happened a couple of years ago with an item I had bought in a major bricks-and-mortar retail chain. After getting home with my new item, I looked at the receipt and realized I had been overcharged. I telephoned the shop. When I eventually got to speak to someone, they told me there was nothing they could do unless I returned to the store. That meant a 24-mile round trip, and I had to wait to be served by a man who did not smile once or apologize for the error. I walked out of the shop with my refund, but it had taken over an hour and I had been made to feel completely negative about the store. I still try to avoid it if I can.

So customer service will inevitably improve at both online and bricks-and-mortar shops, or they will simply be forced out of business by their more considerate competitors.

The need for speed

Some bricks-and-mortar fashion stores proclaim their ability to change their stock every six weeks, because that is a major shift compared with the seasonal changes that used to happen only two or three times a year. Yet online, people are now used to seeing different displays every week, sometimes every day.

Real-world stores can also rarely compete with the speed with which items can be found and bought online. Apart from the traveling time to get to a physical shop in the first place, customers often find that the item they want is not in stock and has to be ordered. A typical retail operator's logistics and distribution system can mean that the item will not be delivered until the next time a lorry is due in, which might be a week away and will involve another trip back to the store. Online, you are able to find what you want, even if it is a rare item, and get it the next day, sometimes even more quickly. People will become more and more used to getting the products they want when they want them, and this can only make the future of online retail even rosier.

Retail will depend on online shopping

There is almost nothing that cannot be sold online. In 2007, Carys Copestake from Manchester in the UK sold her virginity via eBay for £10,000 because she was finding it difficult to pay her university fees. The executive who bought it did not actually take up her offer, but did pay her the money, as he felt sorry for her plight. Also on eBay, Melissa Heuschkel from Connecticut sold the right to name her unborn baby. Online casino Golden Palace paid her $15,500 to name her daughter "Golden Palace Benedetto," or Goldie for short.

And it is not only eBay where you can buy strange items. You can, for instance, get real human skulls at skullsunlimited.com; or if you have plenty of spare cash, you can buy your own island from vladi-private-islands.de.

If people want something, they tend to look online first to see if it can be bought, and generally it can. This means that online customers are becoming increasingly used to finding anything they want, adding it to a shopping cart, and buying it there and then.

So online shopping is clearly popular, but with most shopping still done offline, there continues to be some way to go.

Technology consultancy Gartner has developed a "hype cycle" that plots the interest in technologies over time.[5] Hype cycle theory suggests that all technologies trigger a surge in initial interest leading

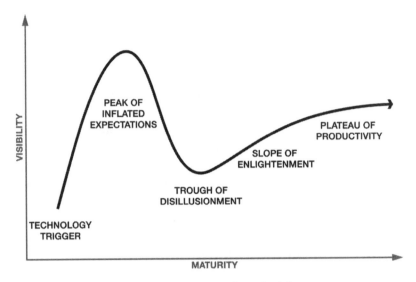

Source: Gartner, Research Methodology
http://www.gartner.com/it/products/research/methodologies/research_hype.jsp

to a "peak of inflated expectations," but as people learn more about the technology and compare it with newer things, it soon plummets into the "trough of disillusionment." As they increase their understanding, they enter the "slope of enlightenment," before really getting to grips with the technology in the "plateau of productivity."

Different technologies take varying amounts of time to go through this typical pattern. The aim of anyone introducing new technology would be to get the product right through to the plateau of productivity as quickly as possible. Nevertheless, some technologies don't make it; they are stuck in the trough of disillusionment forever.

According to Gartner, many aspects of online shopping have yet to reach the plateau of productivity. Indeed, many of the components of a successful online store have not yet even reached the peak of inflated expectations, or are now in the trough of disillusionment. For instance, email marketing is thought to be at its lowest ebb for many years, whereas the use of mobile coupons for special offers is still only on its way up.

The varying acceptance of online shopping technologies only serves to confuse the picture for retailers, making it more difficult to get things right and causing businesses to postpone changes in what they do until the dust settles and the technologies become acceptable. However, all that does is create further delay, because by the time something has reached the plateau of productivity another technology is on its way up to the peak of inflated expectations.

What is worth considering is where online shopping as a whole may be on the hype cycle. Many shoppers remain somewhat skeptical about online retail. This is not helped by incidents such as the delayed deliveries in the run-up to Christmas 2012 experienced by online customers in the UK. Even so, with many countries such as China still only in the foothills of internet shopping, there is considerable global potential to be exploited. Considering all of this, online shopping overall has probably yet to reach the peak of inflated expectations.

Such knowledge can help online retailers plan. It means that they can continue to build online stores and services that truly engage customers. It means that they can experiment with new technologies and see what happens. It means that they know it will be some time before online shopping hits the trough of disillusionment, and by then they should have enough resilience in their systems to overcome this and quickly reach that long-term goal, the plateau of productivity.

And what of bricks and mortar?

Consider for a moment where bricks-and-mortar stores might be on the graph: on their way down to the trough of disillusionment. People are fed up with high parking charges when they visit physical shops and with the cost of fuel. They are increasingly unhappy with the lack of stock and the poor range of items available compared with online shops. And they are dissatisfied with the lack of information and the inability to find things as easily as they do in an internet store. If real-world stores don't fix these fundamental issues they could flounder, leaving the door open for efficient online operations to come in and take even more of their custom.

The beginnings of this have already been witnessed in the demise of many record shops, including HMV, which closed over 100 stores in the UK as online music sales ate into its traditional business. Similarly, photography chain Jessops closed 187 shops when it could no longer cope with the online competition selling digital cameras. However, retail failures like this are not solely due to the rise of online shopping. Indeed, as consultancy firm Aspley said at the beginning of 2012:

> *The internet did not cause these companies to fail. It was the slow rate at which they adapted to the reality of the internet (relative to their competitors) that caused such failure.*[5]

Both HMV and Jessops were subsequently partially rescued, and they are now placing a much greater emphasis on online delivery as they face the future. However, such events do suggest that if traditional retailers do not react quickly to the continuing rise of online shopping, they will carry on being in trouble. All of the psychological advantages of online shopping, such as choice, convenience, product information, and speed, will lead people more and more toward the internet unless bricks-and mortar stores respond and provide the same kind of experience.

Learning from one another

The response from many real-world retailers is to carry on operating their traditional stores because that is what they know. They also offer a printed catalogue for the customers who want it, as well as an online presence. The idea is that this provides people with what they want, through the channel they prefer. However, this "multichannel" retailing is something of a cop-out, taking the easy route instead of dealing with the seismic shift in shopping that is underway.

Many good retailers know this, so they have moved on from multichannel to what is known as "omnichannel." This acknowledges that consumers want to use several different channels at once to gain a complete experience of the retailer. So they may be in a bricks-and-mortar store, carrying their tablet device so they can look at information about specific products, and talking to a sales adviser on their smartphone, all at the same time.

CASE STUDY: CLICK AND COLLECT

In September 2013, eBay and catalogue-based retailer Argos announced a partnership whereby shoppers on eBay would be able to collect the items they had bought from their local Argos store, rather than having it sent by post or courier. This is a novel form of "click and collect" whereby eBay is using what is effectively a rival seller. The scheme only includes 50 of eBay's sellers – and remember that Argos itself has a large store on eBay. What is the attraction for the companies involved?

eBay, of course, increases the level of service and convenience provided to its customers by being able to deliver their purchases in the way they prefer. Argos is presumably expecting increased footfall into its retail stores, from which it may attract additional custom. It is also undoubtedly charging eBay a service fee.

As explained in Chapter 2, customers want delivery on their own terms, so this tie-up certainly helps achieve that. However, the relationship between eBay and Argos also signals something else. It shows that the lines between brands and retailers are becoming blurred as the internet offers a more integrated option for purchasing. That means eBay items being delivered via Argos, Amazon purchases being collected from the local Co-operative store or Staples, and other combinations not even dreamt of yet. The shopper is increasingly in control and retailers need to provide a complete package of services to suit a wide range of individual requirements. They need to think beyond the omnichannel toward an "everywherechannel."

Research shows that people are becoming less loyal to brands, particularly as they become more informed. What shoppers now value most is quality, convenience, and being cared for as individuals. They also increasingly appreciate access to choice and information.

This gives traditional stores a huge opportunity. With the rise in showrooming as a phenomenon, as discussed in Chapter 3, bricks-and-mortar stores that turn themselves into showrooms with web connectivity, online ordering points, and information access through QR codes are going to be doing well. Nevertheless, that's pretty much what the omnichannel provides already. What stores of the future will need are experts: genuinely knowledgeable sales staff who are not merely there to take the money or give superficial advice, but who can provide in-depth information, demonstrate products, and spend time with customers.

If you visit a physical store today often you are ignored, and if you are approached, you may well find that the sales assistant is clueless. You can queue for ages to pay and yet not be greeted with a smile. If this happens, you may prefer to try the company's online store in the future, or even that of a competitor.

Imagine going back to the same shop, having done some online research into what you want to buy. You notice that instead of shelves full of products the store now features cozy places to chat, people drinking coffee, and several touch screens that customers are using. A sales assistant steps toward you and asks what you want, and you explain the product you're interested in buying. The assistant takes you to sit down, offers you a coffee along the way, and chats with you about why you want that product and what you hope it will do for you. While chatting, he has pressed a few keys on his tablet device, which is ordering a sample from the warehouse at the back of the store. As you talk, another assistant turns up with the item you're interested in buying and the first sales assistant demonstrates how to use it. You're allowed to have a play with the product, while the sales assistant suggests you might like to look at a video of people using it. He calls the video up from YouTube on his tablet, then hands the device to you so you can watch. You hand back the tablet and the sales assistant asks you if you have any questions. Sure, you have a couple, and you ask them. You get intelligent, thought-out, well-informed answers; the sales

assistant even prints out a document from the website FAQ section
that contains further information for you.

Does this sound appealing? Do you think it gets sales? You
bet it does – this is the model Apple employs in its iconic stores.

John Lewis department stores in the UK also see the online
and offline worlds as interconnected. Sales generated online are
attributed to the customer's local store rather than to the company's website, meaning that shop staff view the website as an
extension of their own store rather than a competitor.

However, not every retailer needs to turn its bricks-and-
mortar stores into showrooms. The chances are that you won't buy
your groceries this way, for example. And even if clothing retailers are doing clever things with technology, people will still want
to try clothes on. Besides, how would you cope with emergency
purchases, such as a new pair of shoes when your heel snaps? You
wouldn't want to go into a shoe showroom, chat to a shoe expert,
see the shoes you want, but then have to order them online and
wait until they're delivered, meanwhile hobbling around. Showroom
stores will become increasingly popular and they do have a place,
but they will not entirely replace traditional shops.

Indeed, a 2012 study by business consultancy PWC showed
that significant numbers of people still want "old-fashioned" shops
and reported that the notion that "stores will become mainly showrooms in the future" was a myth.[6] The research discovered that
even though many people do research products they want to buy
online, a large proportion of them still want to get the item in a
physical store.

Thus the successful retailers of the future will not focus on
omnichannel or multichannel or online instead of offline, but on
learning from one another and continually adapting to a dynamic
and ever-developing retail environment.

12

CLICK.OLOGY

Consumers behave differently when they shop online than in traditional bricks-and-mortar stores. Understanding these differences, why they occur, and how to exploit this is crucial to online retail success – to demonstrating true click.ology.

Key to this understanding is a recognition of the significance of attention, credibility, perception, self-esteem, social psychology, survival instincts, and trust. These psychological principles drive consumer behavior and underpin the CLICK system on which this book is based.

Convenient: offering real choice and control

There is little doubt that online shopping is convenient. After all, you can do it from the comfort of your own home without having to go out in the cold or the rain. Neither do you have to carry bags and packages back to your car or home on the bus.

However, as I explained in Chapter 2, this is only superficial convenience. Indeed, we can often spend more time shopping online than we do in the real world, so the time saved can be an illusion.

What is far more significant are the deeper psychological elements of convenience, such as the feeling of being in control. One factor that taps into this driver is the vastly broader choice available on- rather than offline. People prefer to choose what they want, rather than what the retailer decides to sell them, and providing a wide choice (or depth of choice in a niche) satisfies this desire.

As a result, an online store that signals either that it has a vast amount of choice or that it services a highly specific sector is likely to perform very well.

Likeable: liking your customers and customers liking you

Customers need to like the online experience of a shop, but unless an internet store demonstrates that it likes its customers, it's on a journey to nowhere. A store needs to appeal to the subtle psycho-logical principle of people liking people who like them.

A good online store shows that it likes its customers by ensuring it is built from their perspective, is focused on their spe-cific needs, and has easy-to-use navigation and an effective search system, as discussed in Chapter 3. The design needs to be right, of course, but the technology behind the site, such as the shopping cart, must also be appropriate, and Chapters 5 and 10 explain how. Furthermore, sharing what they have bought on social networks appeals to people's desire to be liked, so follow the guidelines in Chapter 7 to enable this.

Informative: making things clear

As discussed in Chapter 3, a vast number of online searches for retail products are really looking for information. When an online store includes plenty of information, instead of just products, it sees sales increase: customers can access the depth and level of information relevant to them, and be more sure that they're buying the right product. Customers like sites where they can see a large amount of information. They may not read it all, but it gives them confidence that the online store is useful and that help is there if they want it. Make your site informative and you will be tapping into your customers' desire to be well informed.

Clarity is another aspect of information that enables some online stores to be more successful than others. This means clarity in item descriptions and also in pricing, as discussed in Chapter 4. People expect to know in advance what they are going to pay and to be kept fully informed of additional costs such as tax and ship-ping before they get to the final payment page.

Customized: offering personalized care

In a bricks-and-mortar store, good sales staff are able to make a customer feel that they're being treated as an individual. Indeed, a shop that goes out of its way to do this can charge quite high prices for this very personal approach. Online stores that provide a similar degree of personalization and customization are attractive to customers, as Chapter 6 explains.

But customization online is about much more than simply having a customer's name at the top of a web page once they log in – it is about behind-the-scenes technology that demonstrates the company's care for that customer and offers an online store that can be used the way they want.

Web stores that are customized also offer flexible delivery options determined by what the customer wants, and there are examples of how to achieve this in Chapter 2.

Knowledgeable: gaining trust through expertise

A company that displays deep knowledge about its products and its particular sector is one that buyers tend to trust more, and trust is a key psychological motivator for purchasing. Buyers need confidence that the company supplying them is trustworthy, an issue explored in Chapters 8 and 9.

Generating trust in an online business is also about branding, as explained in Chapter 3, and about the kind of word-of-mouth activity that is generated when a business is known for its expertise. For example, if you wanted to speak to someone who understood the superstore business, you'd feel comfortable talking to someone from Walmart. Similarly, if you wanted to be sure you were buying a computer at the leading edge of design, you would probably start your search at Apple.

The importance of demonstrating knowledge and being a leader in your field is being shown in the omnichannel arena, as discussed in Chapters 3 and 10. New bricks-and-mortar stores are emerging where products are merely "showroomed" – expert sales staff help customers choose the right product, which is then purchased in the online store.

Putting into practice the CLICK system and the wider insights described in this book will help you ensure that you connect and engage with your customers online. Your online store will provide customers with convenience and the freedom to choose exactly what they want. It will appeal to their sense of self and their need to be liked. It will enable customers to be confident that they have chosen the right purchases because they have the relevant information. It will demonstrate care for the customer and adapt its offering to their needs and desires. Finally, it will build trust and authority, providing customers with the certainty that they are buying from a website that really works for them.

NOTES

Chapter 1

1. https://www.learningseed.com/p-400-supermarkets-aisles-of-persuasion.aspx.
2. Graves, P. (2010) *Consumer.ology*, London: Nicholas Brealey Publishing, 132.
3. http://www.dailymail.co.uk/femail/article-419077/Women-spend-years-life-shopping.html.
4. http://newsroom.bmo.com/press-releases/bmo-psychology-of-spending-report-impulse-shoppin-tsx-bmo-201209250821167001.
5. Euromonitor International (2012) *World Retail Data and Statistics*, 7th Edition, London.
6. http://www.psychologytoday.com/blog/sold/201207/what-motivates-impulse-buying.
7. Lane, W. & Manner, C. (2011) The impact of personality traits on smartphone ownership and use, *International Journal of Business and Social Science*, 2(11): 22.
8. http://thenextweb.com/apple/2012/09/14/one-third-americans-want-iphone-5-56-blackberry-users-32-android-users-survey/.
9. Defoe, D. (1726) *The Complete English Tradesman*, London.
10. http://www.davidjones.com.au/About-David-Jones/The-Story-of-David-Jones.
11. Jamal, A., Davies, F.M., Chudry, F., & Al-Marri, M. (2006) Profiling consumers: A study of Qatari consumers' shopping motivations, *Journal of Retailing and Consumer Services*, 13: 67–80.

Chapter 2

1. http://www.aldricharchive.com/snowball.html.
2. American Marketing Association (1984) *Marketing News*, 18(23): 3.
3. Bhatnagar, A., Misra, S., & Raghav Rao, H. (2000) On risk, convenience, and internet shopping behavior, *Communications of the ACM*, 43(11): 98–105.

4. http://www.pewinternet.org/Reports/2008/Online-Shopping.
     aspx.
5. Underhill, P. (2009) *Why We Buy*, New York: Simon & Schuster.
6. Corn, G.J., Chattopadhyay, A., Sengupta, J., & Tripathi, S.
     (2004) Waiting for the web: How screen color affects time per-
     ception, *Journal of Marketing Research*, XLI(May): 215–225.
7. Mowen, J.C. (2004) Exploring the trait of competitiveness
     and its consumer behavior consequences, *Journal of Consumer
     Psychology*, 4: 52–63.
8. http://repub.eur.nl/res/pub/7438/.
9. http://www.memphismuseums.org/sub_exhibit-2590/.
10. Kostecki, M. (1996) Waiting lines as a marketing issue, *European
     Management Journal*, 14(3, June): 295–303.
11. http://www.collectplus.co.uk/.

Chapter 3

1. Jones, G. (1999) *Travel and Holidays on the Internet*, Plymouth:
     Internet Handbooks.
2. Kiel, C.G. & Layton, R.A. (1981) Dimensions of consumer
     information seeking behavior, *Journal of Marketing Research*, 18(2):
     233–239.
3. Case, D.O. (2012) *Looking for Information: A Survey of Research
     on Information Seeking, Needs, and Behaviour*, 3rd edn, Bingley:
     Emerald Group Publishing.
4. Interbrand (2012) *Best Retail Brands 2012*, London: Interbrand.
5. Jansen, B.J., Booth, D.L., & Spink, A. (2007) Determining the
     user intent of web search engine queries, 16th international
     conference on World Wide Web, 1149–1150, New York:
     Association for Computing Machinery.
6. Compete.com (2012) *Seeing between the Lines of the Search and the
     Click*, Boston, MA: Kantar Media.
7. Lau, T. & Horvitz, E. (1999) Patterns of search: Analyzing and
     modeling web query refinement, Proceedings of the seventh
     international conference on User Modeling, 119–128, New York:
     Springer-Verlag.

8. Sub, Q. & Spears, N. (2012) Frustration and consumer evaluation of search advertising and search engine effectiveness, *Journal of Electronic Consumer Research*, 13(2).

9. Martin, C. (2011) *The Third Screen: Marketing to Your Customers in a World Gone Mobile*, London: Nicholas Brealey Publishing.

10. http://www.scribd.com/doc/129119710/Retail-Showrooming-In-Canada-A-report-from-GroupM-Next-and-Catalyst.

11. http://www.tescoplc.com/index.asp?pageid=17&newsid=593.

12. http://www.nellymoser.com/action-codes/qr-codes-retail-stores.

13. http://www.informationweek.co.uk/report-online-shoppers-have-a-4-second-a/193502066.

14. http://www.grahamjones.co.uk/2012/encyclopaedia/psychology-encyclopaedia/eye-tracking.html.

15. Crowder, R.G. & Wagner, R.K. (1992) *The Psychology of Reading*, Oxford: Oxford University Press.

16. Grimes, J. (1996) On the failure to detect changes in scenes across saccades, in K. Akins, *Perception*, Vancouver Studies in Cognitive Science, 2, New York: Oxford University Press, 89–110.

17. http://en.wikipedia.org/wiki/Change_blindness.

18. http://www.nngroup.com/topic/eyetracking/.

19. http://www.nngroup.com/articles/scrolling-and-attention/.

20. Yu, H.H., Chaplin, T.A., Davies, A.J., Verma, R., & Rosa, M.G.P. (2012) A specialized area in limbic cortex for fast analysis of peripheral vision, *Current Biology*, 22(12): 1351–1357.

21. http://www.webcredible.co.uk/blog/checkout-usability-issue.

22. http://www.poynter.org/extra/Eyetrack/.

23. http://www.bbc.co.uk/blogs/thereporters/rorycellanjones/2011/03/world_stores.html.

24. Gullstrand, J. & Jörgensen, C. (2012) Local price competition: The case of Swedish food retailers, *Journal of Agricultural and Food Industrial Organization*, 10(1).

25. Jupiter Research Economic Downturn Online Consumer Survey, Q4 2008.

26. http://www.footfall.com/retail-traffic-global-indices/.

27. http://www.responsenow.com/plans/compare-us-to-the-competition.html.

28. http://www.statista.com/statistics/172685/
    monthly-unique-visitors-of-us-retail-websites/.
29. Heim, G.R. & Kingshuk, K.S. (2001) Operational drivers of
    customer loyalty in electronic retailing: An empirical analysis
    of electronic food retailers, *Manufacturing and Services Operations
    Management*, 3(3): 264.
30. http://www.nytimes.com/2012/09/10/technology/google-
    shopping-competition-amazon-charging-retailers.html.

Chapter 4

1. Wang, Y. & Krishna, A. (2010) Enticing for me but unfair to
    her: Can targeted pricing evoke socially conscious behavior?
    Journal of Consumer Psychology, http://www.sciencedirect.com/
    science/article/pii/S1057740811001070.
2. Huang, J.-H., Chang, C.-T., & Chen, C.Y.-H. (2005) Perceived
    fairness of pricing on the internet, *Journal of Economic Psychology*,
    26(3): 343–361, http://www.sciencedirect.com/science/article/pii/
    S0167487004000558.
3. Thomas, M. & Morwitz, V. (forthcoming) Heuristics in
    numerical cognition: Implications for pricing, in *Handbook
    of Research in Pricing*, London: Edward Elgar; Johnson
    School Research Paper Series No. 1-08, http://ssrn.com/
    abstract=1082885.
4. Eerland, A., Guadalupe, T.M., & Zwaan, R.A. (2011) Leaning
    to the left makes the Eiffel Tower seem smaller: Posture-
    modulated estimation, *Psychological Science*, 22(Dec.): 1511–1514.
5. Switzer, J. (2007) *Instant Income*, New York: McGraw-Hill.
6. Gitomer, J. (2006) *The Little Red Book of Sales Answers*, Upper
    Saddle River, NJ: Prentice Hall.
7. http://www.smeal.psu.edu/cdt/ebrcpubs/res_papers/1999_04.pdf.
8. http://www.valassis.co.uk/PressRelease/
    ac7a6908-docc-4511-b2cc-54f6edc3dc4b.
9. Babukis, E., Tat, P., & Cunningham, W. (1988) Coupon
    redemption: A motivational perspective, *Journal of Consumer
    Marketing*, 5(2): 37–43.

10. http://articles.businessinsider.com/2012-01-26/
    tech/30665968_1_coupon-codes-groupon-online-coupons.
11. Shor, M. & Oliver, R. (2006) Price discrimination through
    online couponing: Impact on likelihood of purchase and
    profitability, *Journal of Economic Psychology*, 27(3): 423–440.
12. Cialdini, R. (1993) *Influence: The Psychology of Persuasion*, New York:
    William Morrow.
13. http://www.youngentrepreneur.com/startingup/startup-business-
    ideas/overcoming-the-groupon-effect-how-to-sell-merchants-on-
    your-start-up-deal-site/.
14. http://www.nielsen.com/us/en/newswire/2011/deal-with-it-
    discounts-drive-brand-love-on-social-media.html.
15. http://www.marketingmagazine.co.uk/article/1156500/
    Email-marketing-approval-ratings-hit-time-high-claims-research.
16. Teena, B. & Abhishek, S. (2012) A study of viral marketing
    phenomenon: Special reference to videos and e-mails,
    International Journal of Marketing and Management Research, 3(5):
    37–49.
17. Harmon, S.K. & Hill, C.J. (2003) Gender and coupon use,
    Journal of Product and Brand Management, 12(3): 166–179.
18. Adcock, P. (2011) *Supermarket Shoppology, Shopping Behaviour*,
    Tamworth: Xplained.
19. http://on.wsj.com/12KASoC.
20. Kannanm, P.K. & Kopalle, P.K. (2001) Dynamic pricing on the
    internet: Importance and implications for consumer behavior,
    International Journal of Electronic Commerce, 5(3): 63–83.
21. http://anzmac.info/conference/2007/papers/McKechnie_2.pdf.
22. http://www.cepr.org/meets/wkcn/6/6680/papers/Aguzzoni.pdf.

Chapter 5

1. http://baymard.com/lists/cart-abandonment-rate.
2. http://www.internetretailer.com/2012/04/06/
   most-e-retailers-give-when-shoppers-abandon-carts.
3. http://seewhy.com/blog/2012/10/10/97-shopping-cart-
   abandonment-rate-mobile-devices-concern-you/.

4. http://econsultancy.com/uk/blog/10052-free-shipping-and-delivery-timing-are-key-for-customer-satisfaction.
5. Ariely, D. (2009) Predictably Irrational, London: HarperCollins.
6. http://unbounce.com/conversion-rate-optimization/case-study-your-slow-shopping-cart-pages-are-killing-conversions-heres-what-you-can-do-about-it/.
7. http://www.wordstream.com/blog/ws/2011/08/23/page-speed-conversion-rate-optimization.
8. http://blog.kissmetrics.com/loading-time/.
9. http://www.qubitproducts.com/services/research/page/2/.
10. http://www.marketingsherpa.com/article/new-ecommerce-research-website-tactics.
11. http://www.forbes.com/sites/georgeanders/2012/04/04/bezos-tips/.
12. http://blog.rejoiner.com/2012/06/amazon-shopping-cart-experience/.

Chapter 6

1. http://www.success.com/articles/391-how-i-do-it-tony-hsieh-zappos-com.
2. http://www.ft.com/cms/s/0/98240e90-39fc-11e0-a441-00144feabdc0.html.
3. http://www.sciencedirect.com/science/article/pii/S0925527313001291.
4. http://www.dpreview.com/forums/post/37246032.
5. http://www.independent.co.uk/life-style/gadgets-and-tech/features/ipad-manual-not-included-1956027.html.
6. http://media.stellaservice.com/public/pdf/Customer_Experience_Impact_North_America.pdf.
7. http://www.synthetix.com/website_documents/Synthetix_Online_Customer_Service_Survey_2012.pdf.
8. http://youtu.be/Y-pDjKAjV1g.
9. Stromhetz, D.B., Rind, B., Fisher, R., & Lynn, M. (2002) Sweetening the till: The use of candy to increase restaurant tipping, Journal of Applied Social Psychology, 32(2): 300–309.
10. Joinson, A., McKenna, K., Postmes, T., & Reips, U.-D. (eds.) (2009) The Oxford Handbook of Internet Psychology, Oxford: Oxford University Press, 245–247.

11. http://www.eloqua.com/resources/marketing-insights/optimal-number-of-form-fields.html.
12. Smith, J.L. (2012) *Relevant Selling*, New York: Executive Suite Press.

Chapter 7

1. http://nytmarketing.whsites.net/mediakit/pos/.
2. Alicke, M.D. (1992) Complaining behavior in social interaction, *Personality and Social Psychology Bulletin*, 18(3): 286–295.
3. Meerman Scott, D. (2010) *Real Time Marketing and PR*, Hoboken, NJ: John Wiley.
4. http://www.internetretailer.com/2013/02/08/google-spurs-retailers-use-google.

Chapter 8

1. Coker, B.L. (2012) Seeking the opinions of others online: Evidence of evaluation overshoot, *Journal of Economic Psychology*, 33(6): 1033–1042.
2. http://www.redorbit.com/news/science/1112728587/instinct-intellect-decisions-tel-aviv-university-110912/.

Chapter 9

1. Salerno, S. (2005) *SHAM*, London: Nicholas Brealey Publishing.
2. Kamins, M.A., Folkes, V.S., & Fedorikhin, A. (2009) Promotional bundles and consumers' price judgements; When the best things in life are not free, *Journal of Consumer Research*, 36(4): 660–670.
3. http://cwru-daily.com/news/psychology-research-finds-surprise-win-or-loss-impacts-likelihood-of-risk-taking/.
4. http://en.wikipedia.org/wiki/Milgram_experiment.
5. http://www.bleepingcomputer.com/virus-removal/remove-fbi-anti-piracy-warning-ransomware.
6. http://pro.sagepub.com/content/52/6/557.short.

7. Bahr, G.S. & Ford, R.A. (2011) How and why pop-ups don't work: Pop-up prompted eye movements, user affect and decision making, *Computers in Human Behavior*, 27(2): 776–783.
8. Dunn, B. (2012) Gut feelings and the reaction to perceived inequity, *Cognitive, Affective, and Behavioral Neuroscience*, 12(3): 419–429.
9. http://www.psychologytoday.com/blog/ulterior-motives/201109/the-upside-and-downside-envy.

Chapter 10

1. Underhill, P. (2009) *Why We Buy*, New York: Simon & Schuster.
2. http://www.staff.uni-mainz.de/oberfeld/wine2.html.

Chapter 11

1. Conor, D. (2006) *Managing at the Speed of Change*, New York: Villard Books.
2. http://www.thedrum.com/news/2013/01/04/research-shows-almost-half-all-clothing-purchases-made-online-are-returned-january.
3. http://www.smartplanet.com/blog/bulletin/how-to-hug-a-chicken-taste-bitterness-via-the-internet/3958.
4. http://www.gartner.com/technology/research/methodologies/hype-cycle.jsp.
5. http://www.aspleyconsultants.co.uk/why-do-some-high-street-brands-fail-and-others-thrive-clue-its-not-because-of-the-internet/.
6. http://www.pwc.com/gx/en/retail-consumer/retail-consumer-publications/global-multi-channel-consumer-survey/country-snapshots.jhtml.

INDEX

ACKNOWLEDGMENTS

A book like this is not written without help; it might have my name on the cover, but inevitably there are several people and companies who have helped me produce it. I am grateful to the research from eMarketer, Euromonitor, and Statistica. I am also grateful to Derek Arden, Andrew Dyster, Frank Furness, Lawrence McGinty, Nigel Morgan, and Philip Webb, who have all allowed me to use material about them. I would like to thank my clients over the years who have spurred me on to find out more about the psychology of online shoppers. My colleagues at the Professional Speaking Association have been supportive too, encouraging me to write this book, and I thank them all for the advice they have given me. The individuals who have filled in research surveys and polls I have conducted have also helped by giving me useful insights into what online shoppers think. Obviously, my publishers have been very encouraging; in particular I'd like to thank Susannah Lear, who first encouraged me to write *Click.ology*, Nicholas Brealey himself, who has been tremendously helpful throughout the process of writing this book, and my editor, Sally Lansdell. My most heartfelt thanks must go to my family. I would like to thank my wife who has let me hide away in my office for hours on end, tapping away at my keyboard. But my biggest thanks are devoted to my 13-year-old son Elliot, who kept poking his head around the office door trying not to interrupt, but keen to find out how it was going and constantly encouraging me to type some more.

Graham Jones
Reading, Berkshire
October 2013

CLICK.OLOGY.BIZ

Further information about Click.ology can be found at

http://click.ology.biz

On the website, you will find:

- ◆ Links to the references and sources used in this book.
- ◆ Further useful information extending the material in this book.
- ◆ Summaries of each chapter.

Furthermore, you will be able to find out details of Click.ology "CLICK" workshops and masterclasses for businesses wanting to sell more online. There is also material about the Click.ology consultancy service, which helps retailers develop a successful strategy based on an understanding of the behavior of their particular customers, using "CLICK," the Click.ology five-step process.

Click.ology.biz includes free downloadable guides on various aspects of online retail, such as "How to choose shopping cart software" and "How to benefit from social selling."

For these free guides and more, please visit:

http://click.ology.biz